Jerry Mushin held academic posts for forty-five years until he retired in 2015. He also taught in a prison, a police training college, government departments, and for professional bodies. His academic writing, which is principally in the areas of monetary policy and exchange rates, has been published in Australia, Greece, India, Japan, Netherlands, New Zealand, Nigeria, Qatar, Singapore, Switzerland, the United Kingdom, and the United States. He is the author of undergraduate textbooks, a novel, and children's stories. A Chinese translation of one of his textbooks has been published in Beijing. He has contributed articles to newspapers in several countries and to the *Encyclopedia of Economic and Business History*.

First published by Piwaiwaka Press 2024
www.piwaiwakapress.com
163 Rata Street, Naenae
Lower Hutt 5011
New Zealand
ISBN 978-1-0670286-2-6
All rights reserved.

Copyright © Jerry Mushin 2024
Cover Artwork: Alan Benge
Cover Layout: Madden Hay

Jerry Mushin asserts his right to be known as the author of this work. This book is copyright. Except for the purposes of fair review, no part of this book may be stored or transmitted or reproduced in any form or by any means, electronic or mechanical, including recording or storage in any information retrieval system, without permission in writing from the publisher.

An Unlikely Academic

Jerry Mushin

This book celebrates the joys, frustrations, absurdities, pleasures, friendliness, enthusiasm, injustices, humour, contradictions, and poignancy of my academic experience. I am grateful to my teachers and colleagues, and especially to my students, from whom I have learnt an immense amount. I also thank my wife Claudia and our son Stephen for their encouragement.

Although this book is based on my experience, some parts of it are truer than others, and neither individuals nor institutions are named. This is to avoid embarrassing or offending a large number of former colleagues and an enormous number of former students. It is also because the book is only partly about the places and the people that I remember. It is also about the significant evolution of the tertiary education system that has occurred in the UK and in New Zealand (and in other countries) since the 1960s, and especially since the 1980s.

Some of the content of this book has been published in my articles in the *Jamaica Observer*.

Contents

1 Medical Prologue	9
2 A New Start	14
3 Research Assistant	22
4 Lecturer in Economics	29
5 Meetings. Meetings. Meetings	36
6 First Conference Presentation	43
7 Information Evening	48
8 Experienced Lecturer	54
9 A New Country	62
10 Lecturing again	68
11 Diminished Connections	75
12 Happy Families	82
13 Mutual Respect	89
14 Know Your Colleagues	96
15 Communication and Language	102
16 Life after University	109
17 Conflicts of Interest	116
18 Curing Brain Murk	123
19 Textbook Issues	129
20 Academic Publications	136
21 Explosive Growth of Marketing	142
22 Exit from Academia	148
Appendix	153

1
Medical Prologue

When I was fourteen years old, I decided that I wanted to be a doctor. I do not remember how I reached this conclusion. All I can say is that it seemed like a good idea at the time.

My parents were pleased. My mother told her hairdresser, 'My son is going to be a doctor'. My teachers were more measured in their response. They told me that medical training was very demanding. They were too polite to tell me that the other aspiring doctors at my school were academic heavyweights, which I was not. But, of course, I knew this. The average of my test marks that was entered in each of my end-of-term reports always placed me near the bottom of the class. However, I had made my decision, and I was not going to be deterred.

Some of my peers had difficulty choosing their sixth-form subjects, but not me. For admission to a medical school, it had to be chemistry, physics, and biology. These were not easy subjects for me. I found the mathematical aspects of chemistry and physics particularly tiresome. Friends who had chosen history and economics found their studies much more engaging, but I ignored their enthusiasm.

I was interviewed at a London medical school. This was an uncomfortable fifteen minutes. I was asked to name a famous doctor and explain why I found his work inspiring. I said I did not know of any famous doctors. The three interviewers laughed. They laughed a lot during my interview. I do not remember many of the other questions. At the end of the interview, I felt that I was a failure. To my surprise, I was admitted to the medical school.

I studied intensely for my seventh-form exams, and I passed in all subjects. My grades were undistinguished, which means that I nearly failed.

For almost three months, between my last exam and the start of the university year, I worked as a hospital porter. [Hospital porters are now known as orderlies.] I wanted to get some useful experience. This job was interesting and mostly enjoyable, but it also taught me how little I knew about the career that I had chosen. Some parts of the work were disturbing. I was especially affected by the small children, imprisoned alone in their cots, who sobbed and sobbed and sobbed and sobbed and who appeared to have been abandoned. The nurses were often too busy to comfort them.

My duties included pushing unconscious patients on trolleys from wards to operating theatres and *vice versa*. Occasionally, I had to assist with transferring exceptionally heavy patients from and onto trolleys. Other tasks were less emotionally demanding. I pushed trolleys containing hot meals from the kitchens to the wards. I pushed trolleys containing dirty dishes from the wards to the kitchens. I delivered mail around the hospital. I removed rubbish. I pushed patients in wheel-chairs from taxis to their out-patient appointments and back again. I took my turn at making tea for the other porters.

Hospital procedures often surprised me (although, of course, many of these have now changed). Every time that I took a patient in a wheel-chair from a ward to the x-ray department, I was handed a brown folder of notes. And, every time, I was told, 'Don't let the patient handle the notes'. The third time this happened, I asked, 'Why not?' 'Because he might read them,' said the nurse.

In October 1966, I started the first year of my medical-school course. There were eighty students in the class, of whom seven were female. In addition to lectures in anatomy, physiology, biochemistry, and other subjects, there were laboratory sessions, tutorials, and, of course, dissection. There was not much time for reflection.

The dissection room was a daunting place. There was a large number of bodies (known as cadavers) on tables, and each was assigned to a small group of students. During the year, we followed a detailed manual, and we dissected the whole of a human body. The arm and the leg were dissected in the first term, the thorax and abdomen in the second term, and the head and neck in the third term. I have a very clear memory of my first morning in the dissection room. I recall making the initial incisions that exposed the *deltoid* (shoulder) muscle and the *latissimus dorsi* (back) muscle. Like many of the students in the class, I did not enjoy dissection.

I wanted to do well and, initially, I devoted several hours each evening to study, but it gradually became a burden. Every nerve, every muscle, and every blood vessel (and every tributary of every blood vessel) had a name. Every bump and every kink in every structure had a name. All these names, which usually had many syllables, had to be learnt. There was an enormous amount to be learnt in the other subjects too. There were frequent tests, in which I did not achieve high marks.

My medical studies were a serious disappointment. It is difficult to explain how serious it was. It was deeply disturbing that I had to spend long hours memorising enormous amounts of factual information. This was not as I expected university study to be. I could find no interest in some of the subjects, and not much interest in the others.

And I no longer wanted to be a doctor.

To my great embarrassment, I fell asleep several times in histology (microscopic anatomy) lectures. This was due to boredom not tiredness. Other students were also asleep, but this did not reassure me. The conditions in the lecture theatre did not encourage students to be attentive. The air was warm and still. Blackout blinds were lowered, and these allowed absolutely no light to enter. In total darkness, in which I was unable to take notes because I could not see my hand holding my pen, we were shown a series of slides of human tissues taken from microscopes. These were in shades of pale grey. They all looked much the same to me. And the lecturer's presentation style was as boring as the material that he showed us.

I remember a meeting in April with one of the professors. I had sought his advice because I was increasingly uneasy about the course that I was doing and about the type of work that it would lead to. I was thinking of withdrawing from the course. He told me to keep a stiff upper lip. He also told me not to flinch. He had got nowhere by flinching. He talked about bridges. He told me to cross my bridges when I got to them. He told me not to burn my bridges. He also advised me to advance, on a narrow front, deep into enemy territory. He gave me the same advice again and again and again and again, often in the same words. I have forgotten most of the content of this lengthy conversation, but I recall that I contributed a small proportion of the words that were spoken. I tried to follow the advice that I was given, but this was a bad decision. I should have withdrawn immediately.

However, I did not withdraw immediately. I trudged onward and trudged onward and onward and onward. Life became hard. I failed the end-of-year exams. This was not enjoyable.

My mother was very disappointed.

'What shall I say happened to you?'
'Say that I failed my exams.'
'Oh dear.'

In September 1967, I started a course leading to a degree in economics. I should have done this a year earlier.

My mother found my choice troubling. 'What sort of work do economics graduates do?' I could not answer this question, which made her even more troubled.

2
A New Start

After failing my medical-school exams, I decided, within a couple of days, that my next objective would be to get a degree in economics. I had been thinking about this, intermittently and only vaguely, for several months but without taking myself seriously. Suddenly, there was a feeling of urgency. I contacted the Universities Central Council on Admissions, which processed the admission of students to undergraduate courses at universities (but not polytechnics), and was told that, in the academic year that was about to begin, there were no places remaining in university courses in economics. [From 1993, the UCCA's successor, with an expanded role, was the Universities and Colleges Admissions Service.]

I then sought information about undergraduate courses in non-university institutions. I enrolled at a polytechnic in a provincial city on a course leading to a degree of the University of London. In the lexicon that was used by the University at that time, this made me an External student. [Students at the constituent institutions (including twelve medical schools) of the University were defined as Internal students]. The polytechnics were not involved in the assessment of External students. Undergraduate exams were set and marked by the University. The syllabuses were specified by the University. External students were entitled to use

University services, including the careers advice service and the library, but, since these were almost two hundred miles away, this was of doubtful benefit to me.

In the 1960s, the higher education system in the UK comprised the universities and the others, which were generally known as polytechnics. Publicity material (or, perhaps, propaganda) from the Ministry of Education stated that institutions in the two sectors had 'parity of esteem', but nobody believed this. Students on undergraduate courses at polytechnics had generally been refused places at universities. They assumed, probably correctly, that most of their lecturers had failed to find jobs at universities.

Partly to cater for the 'baby-boom' generation, and partly to avoid some of the costs of establishing new universities, undergraduate education had been expanded by changing the functions of institutions that had been teaching at lower levels. Sadly, the funding was inadequate. In most cases, the buildings were too small, and the staff were overworked.

Non-university institutions did not have the authority to award degrees. They were not entitled to issue academic money. In the late 1960s, courses for External students of the University of London were gradually being replaced by courses supervised and validated by the Council for National Academic Awards (founded in 1965). This allowed the polytechnics to have much greater involvement (but not autonomy) in the assessment of students and in the preparing of syllabuses. The CNAA was required to ensure that its degrees were of the same standard as the degrees awarded by universities. The UK polytechnics became universities in the early 1990s, which meant that they acquired the authority to award their own degrees. The CNAA was abolished in 1993.

Even on the first day of the course, it was obvious that

my experience as an economics student was going to be different from my experience as a medical student. There were thirty students in the class. Eight students were female, more than three times the proportion in my medical-school class, but this was not the most significant change. Almost all the students had failed exams, and some had failed many exams. A large proportion of the students, including me, had failed university courses. Some of the students had needed several attempts at their sixth-form exams to accumulate enough passes to be admitted. The other immediately obvious difference was that, as at my primary and secondary schools but unlike my medical-school class, there were students of minority races.

The polytechnic buildings were inelegant, converted from other uses, crowded, and often shabby, cold, and draughty. This made them very different from the medical-school buildings that I had attended. It also made them very different from the magnificent buildings of the university in the same city.

I was determined not to fail a second time so, like the other students, I took my studies seriously. I was frequently aware that I did not know the jargon of economic theory. The students who had passed sixth-form economics, or who had failed university exams in economics, were clearly ahead of me. The type of study was also unfamiliar. Although facts needed to be retained, the emphasis was on understanding theory, including different approaches, and not on the learning (and reciting) of thousands of facts.

I recall the first essay that I wrote as an economics student. Having chosen science subjects in the sixth form, this was the first time that I had been asked to write an essay. I had not understood the nature of an essay. In addition, although I did not know this, my understanding of some of the theory was superficial and muddled. On my essay, the lecturer wrote, "This is rubbish. I shall not be surprised if you fail your exams". This was an abrupt and unpleasant awakening. However, after much effort, and guidance from other students, my subsequent essays were more successful. I also benefitted from the help and support that I received from my lecturers, who were knowledgeable in their subjects and exceptionally good teachers.

In addition to compulsory subjects in each year of the course, options were chosen from a list. My choices included mathematics, which I found difficult, but which I thought might give me useful skills. Unfortunately, economic history was a popular option and so there were no places left. I also chose sociology, public finance, and political history. These subjects were rewarding, partly because of the lecturers' enthusiasm. Compulsory subjects included the history of political thought, which was initially an irritant. I found little interest in the writings of Aristotle and Socrates. However, more recent writers, including Machiavelli, Hobbes, Rousseau, Mill, and Marx, held my attention. This subject encouraged me to continue reading in this area after I graduated, which I would probably not have done if I had completed my medical degree.

All five of the three-hour Part One exams at the end of the first year had to be passed to proceed to the rest of the course. There were eight three-hour Part Two exams at the end of the third year. Two of the Part Two exams were on the same day. All the exams were set by the University of London. They were also invigilated by the University. The invigilators, who were probably retired academics, wore gowns and carried large briefcases marked "University of London" in one-inch gold letters.

Exam results were sent to candidates by post. Students

who were impatient to receive this information could get it several weeks earlier in London. We were told that at midday, on the prescribed date, the results would be posted on a glass-fronted notice board outside the Senate House, the administrative headquarters of the University of London. Of course, I went to London, after both the Part One exams and the Part Two exams, to get my results.

For my Part One results, I arrived at the Senate House at 11.55. I was amazed at the size of the crowd that was already there, and more were arriving every minute. There were about six hundred External candidates for the economics degree Part One exams that year and it looked like most of them were there. Precisely at 12 noon, as the St Pancras Church clock chimed the hour, the heavy doors of the Senate House were opened and a man carrying a large briefcase walked about fifty yards towards the notice board. He was accompanied by two supporters. The crowd parted to let them through. I watched from the back of the crowd. Fortunately, there was a park bench to stand on, or I would have seen nothing. The glass front of the notice board was slowly unlocked. Then, also slowly, several sheets of paper were pinned to the board and the glass front carefully closed and locked. The three men retreated. Again, the crowd parted to let them through. Then the crowd surged forward. Everyone wanted to see the notice board, but the people at the board did not want to leave. It was a good-natured crowd and there was no aggressive behaviour, but everyone wanted to see the board and those who had already reached it did not want to leave. It was forty minutes before I got close enough to read the typewritten notice.

I was expecting the notice to be a list of names, but it showed only students' examination numbers. It was an enormous relief that my number was included in the list.

When I went to London to get the result of my Part

Two exams, I arrived at the Senate House an hour early. Hundreds of people were there before me. Just like two years earlier, it was about forty minutes after the notice was placed on the board that I was near enough to read it. The Part Two results were divided into First, Upper Second, Lower Second, and Third Class Honours, and Pass. I was very worried about my performance in the exams, and I was expecting to get a Pass degree (or a failure). Although I had a nagging feeling that it was undeserved, it was an enormous pleasure to be awarded a degree with Lower Second Class Honours.

When I was a medical student, like most of my classmates who were not living at their parents' homes, I lived in lodgings (known as digs). My landlady was friendly and kind, but she was still a landlady. This is always an awkward relationship. However well-meaning the landlady, you are still living in the spare bedroom of someone else's house. And many landladies found it difficult not to take on a mothering role in relation to their young lodgers. When I became an economics student, I briefly lived in lodgings because I was in an unfamiliar city where I knew no-one. However, I quickly moved into a flat shared with other students. Although relationships with flatmates can sometimes be difficult, this was a much better arrangement. In addition to the obvious practicalities, it encouraged the making of real friends.

One of my flatmates, with whom I am still in contact more than fifty years later, was a law student. He was finding his studies to be unengaging. He used stronger language than this, but that is what he meant. Some evenings, I discussed with him the lectures I had attended that day. I also showed him my textbooks. He got interested in the content of my course. He was also interested in my experience as a medical student, and he could see similarities with his situation. Eventually, he decided to abandon his law studies and enrol for a degree in economics. I did not intend to convert him. I had no wish to be a missionary. Nevertheless, the outcome was pleasing. He successfully completed his economics course. The obvious conclusion is that higher education should be demanding but not a drudgery. Square pegs need to be in square holes.

Preparing for my exams was stressful. Although essays and other assignments were written by External students, and marked by their lecturers, they were not part of the assessment. Everything depended on the exams. A few weeks before my Part Two exams, I solemnly promised myself that, once my degree had been awarded, I would never sit another exam. I have not ignored that pledge.

In October 1969, at the start of my last year as a student, I applied for numerous jobs. I did not want to be in a boring job (or unemployed) at the end of my course. I applied to banks, insurance companies, manufacturing companies, and other employers of economics graduates. Many of these applications led to interviews, and I was offered several jobs. However, after some of the interviews, I withdrew my applications.

I remember clearly the interviewer who suddenly said, 'Have you got a pair of scissors that I can borrow?'

'What size do you need?'

'Hurrah', he said, 'you've passed that test, with distinction'.

Although the interview was a success, and I was promised that an employment contract would be sent to me within a few days, I withdrew that application for employment that afternoon.

I also applied to universities and polytechnics for a place to study for a postgraduate degree by thesis. I was not willing to attempt another exam, but pursuing a research project, with expert supervision, was appealing.

In November 1969, I was interviewed at one of the universities that had been founded in the 1960s. This was a beautiful modern spacious campus, which was a stark contrast to the polytechnic where I was a student (which was neither beautiful nor modern nor spacious nor a campus). The outcome was a salaried job as a Research Assistant, starting in August 1970. I would be assisting one of the professors. I would also be undertaking my own research project and writing a thesis. I am unable to explain how pleased I was at this opportunity (especially with a salary). The worry was that the offer was conditional on my being awarded a degree with Second Class Honours. I was not confident that this would happen (and neither were my lecturers).

I found employment each summer in department stores while I was a student. I sold garden furniture, lampshades, and other goods, and operated lifts. I also sold carpets at a discount warehouse whose slogan, in daily newspapers and on each of its shop-windows, was 'The more you spend, the more you save. Come on in!' These jobs were interesting but only because they lasted just a few weeks. I also worked as a postman. I enjoyed being outdoors, but the suburban streets were empty and silent at 6.00am, when my first delivery began, and it was solitary and lonely work. It was even worse in heavy rain. My summer jobs were neither difficult nor tedious, but I was pleased when they ended. Having been awarded a degree meant that I could leave such work behind.

3
Research Assistant

I started my job as a Research Assistant with enthusiasm but also with some trepidation. I was not certain that I had the right skills for the job, partly because I did not know what skills I would need. I had only a hazy understanding of the nature of the work that I would be doing. However, I knew that this job was an opportunity, and I was not going to waste it.

Within a few days, it was obvious that my undergraduate studies were less relevant than my interviewer, whose assistant I had become, had anticipated. My mathematical and statistical skills were nowhere near as good as his. I did not know the meanings of many of the technical words that he used, but it was worse than that. I had no memory of ever hearing (or reading) these words before. He was able to think aloud in algebra (and even in trigonometry), at conversational speed, but I could not. I needed my algebra (and especially my trigonometry) to be in writing, and I needed to take it slowly (and preferably in silence).

I also had no experience of using computers. Computers were not used, or even mentioned, in my undergraduate course. This was not a good preparation for my new job.

I was grateful that my younger colleagues were generous with their time and taught me useful theory and techniques in mathematics and statistics. Computing staff, who were brimming with enthusiasm, energy, and kindness, helped me to learn many of the skills that I needed. But I still felt awkward.

The professor that I was employed to assist was also the supervisor of my thesis. He had very precise ideas about how I should proceed with my research project. I welcomed this because I had no relevant experience, but my relationship with him was not as good as I had expected. Although he always tried to be sympathetic and friendly, he sometimes found my lack of experience to be exasperating.

My work often consisted of retrieving large amounts of data, usually from government sources but also from the private sector and using the university computer to run statistical analyses of this. This was not as interesting as I thought it was going to be. I had to write a description and discussion of each of the trends that I had identified. Then I waited to be summoned to hear the response. I usually got the analysis right, but I remember the times when I did not. Sometimes I had used the wrong statistical technique. Sometimes I had used the correct technique, but my interpretation of the results made it look like I had not understood the theoretical process (which was not surprising because I had not).

I spent many hours punching holes in paper tape, which was how data was inputted into the computer. It was 1970, and this was the latest technology. I sat at a keyboard, and I typed thousands of numbers. As I did this, the numbers appeared on paper, and holes were punched in narrow paper tape. The sound of the machine was loud and monotonous and, after a few hours, oppressive. The paper tape was not of robust quality, and it was easy to tear. It needed careful handling, but I eventually learnt how to avoid tearing the tape.

Mistakes on the keyboard were more serious. When I

typed an incorrect figure, I would mark with pencil the incorrect holes on the tape. Then I would continue typing, perhaps for several hours, until I reached the end of the data. I would feed the tape back into the machine and duplicate the holes onto another tape. I would watch the first tape moving slowly through the machine until my pencil mark became visible. I needed to stop the tape just before the pencil mark entered the machine, then type the correct data, manually move the first tape just past the error, and continue the duplication of the holes on the rest of the tape. None of this was difficult. It was just wearisome and boring, and it took hours and hours and hours.

Each day, I spent many hours sitting at the punched-tape machine and trying not to listen to the monotony and oppression of its sound. If I had failed my exams, I reminded myself wryly, I would not have been allowed to do this work.

I rented a room in a shared house. There were ten of us living in a late-Victorian mansion. The small rooms on the top floor were probably intended for servants, and I had one of those. I paid less rent than the people who had the much larger rooms on the other floors. This was a good way to make some contacts in an unfamiliar city, but there were necessarily stresses. For example, there were only two bathrooms, which, especially at peak washing times, was not enough.

I then moved to a small town about twenty miles from the university. I rented a cottage in the grounds of a large house that had been built in about 1820. This was the groom's quarters, attached to the stables. My landlord, who lived in the large house, was a doctor. For older people, who had known him since he was at primary school in the town, he was "the doctor". Everyone knew the doctor. I was in a shop near the cottage, when I had lived there a few days, when one of my neighbours introduced me to her son and grandson as 'the young man in the doctor's cottage'. I had always lived in big cities, and mostly in bland suburbs, so this was a refreshing social environment. It was particularly interesting because, for many years, I had assumed that I was going to become a doctor in a small town.

Postgraduate students were invited (or encouraged) to become part-time tutors. This work was paid, although not generously. Although I was a salaried employee, this included me. I agreed to take two first-year tutorials per week. This was enjoyable and worthwhile. Some of the students found their lectures difficult. When they mimicked their lecturers, I could understand why. They said that my tutorials did not merely help them to understand the lectures, they made the lectures redundant. I was fortunate that the lecturers who had taught me had (mostly) been outstanding teachers, so I knew the best way to explain theory to eighteen-year-olds. The students in my tutorial groups were always responsive and friendly. Some of the students also told me things about my supervisor and his colleagues that they probably did not want me to know. My tutorials rapidly became more rewarding than the rest of my work.

Word-processing computers were not available (and would not become readily available for more than fifteen years) so I submitted handwritten reports. When I was a student, all my essays and assignments were handwritten. None of my classmates owned a typewriter. Despite my efforts to improve it, my handwriting was not, and had never been, elegant, neat, or even easily legible. My supervisor said nothing about this when he read the first document that I gave him, but the meaning of his grimaces was easy to guess. He refused to read my second document. He handed it back to me with a flourish. 'Look, this is impossible to read. Ask one of the secretaries to type it. Tell her it's urgent and tell her I want it done by tomorrow morning.'

This incident reminded me that my handwriting had been a problem since I was a child. When I was seven years old, following persistent untidy work, my teacher made me stay indoors to repeat my writing when the other children went out to play. This punishment did not lead to an improvement in my handwriting. It merely made me dislike that teacher.

I was worried that my difficult handwriting might complicate my relationship with my supervisor so, that afternoon, I bought a typewriter. Some of my academic colleagues were impressed, but only cautiously. They warned me that typing was not as easy as it looked. They were right. It took me longer than I thought it would to become reasonably proficient, but it was worth the effort. It impressed my supervisor. It also impressed me because, for the first time, my work was easy to read. After a few weeks, I could type faster than I could write, which was a special bonus.

My research topic had to be chosen in consultation with, and approved by, my supervisor. I had no experience of academic research, and my suggestions were tentative and not adequately thought out. My supervisor was not impressed by my ideas. He told me why, and, of course, he was right. The easy solution was to let him choose a topic. When he told me what he wanted me to do, I was not certain that it would be interesting, but I did not say this.

I worked hard on my research project. I followed my supervisor's advice. I carefully noted his comments on the work that I submitted to him. I did everything that he advised me to do. I accumulated interesting results, and I planned my thesis. I wrote and wrote and wrote. It gradually took shape. Sadly, it got less and less rewarding. I increasingly had the feeling that the whole exercise was almost pointless. But I pressed on, regardless.

I had a two-year fixed-term employment contract as a Research Assistant. After a little over one year, I started applying for jobs. I could feel the end of the contract approaching. I had particularly liked tutoring, so I read *The Times Higher Education Supplement* and *The Guardian* and submitted applications for advertised lecturing posts at universities and polytechnics. Months later, having had a few interviews but no offers of employment, I began to get worried. I did not want to be without a job, and I did not want to be in an unrewarding job. Several of the friends that I had known when I was an economics student, and who were now working in the private sector, had sent me dreary pessimistic letters describing how tedious their work was. This was a worrying time for me. Then a surprising thing happened. Although I had not requested it, I was offered a one-year extension to my employment contract. This was good news indeed for three reasons. It was encouraging that I was not the failure that I sometimes thought I was, I was more likely to be able to complete my thesis satisfactorily if I was at the same university as my supervisor, and I was not about to be unemployed.

In my third year as a Research Assistant, I was determined to finish my thesis. This work now held very little interest and had become a boring and tedious grind, but I listened to my supervisor's advice, and I followed it. Towards the end of that year, I accepted the offer of a lecturing post at a polytechnic. This was a permanent employment contract. I had not applied for any jobs that were advertised as short-term contracts and I was beginning to wonder whether this was an unwise decision.

I submitted my thesis, in the required hard-back binding with gold lettering on the cover, just before starting my new job. It was many weeks before I was invited to attend an oral exam. This lasted more than an hour and it did not go well. I waited many more weeks before receiving the verdict.

The examiners decided that my thesis was not good enough. I was intensely disappointed but, of course, I knew that they were right. I was told that I would be allowed to submit a revised thesis within three months. I decided to do this. However, since my new job was interesting and demanding, I did not start revising my thesis immediately. I postponed this work, and postponed it, and postponed it, and postponed it. I concentrated my efforts on my new job. Eventually I stopped thinking about my thesis.

Then I received a letter from the registrar of the university where I had worked as a Research Assistant. He wrote that, since I had missed the three-month deadline, my name would be 'deleted from the register of postgraduate students at this university'. If I had asked for additional time, it would probably have been granted, but I did not do this. My thesis had become an ugly memory that I wanted to forget.

4
Lecturer in Economics

My new job, as a Lecturer in Economics, began a month after I accepted the offer of employment. I was impatient to start this new role. My Research Assistant job had become onerous. Although I had no teaching qualification, and no experience of public speaking, I knew I was going to enjoy lecturing.

The polytechnic was in an industrial city whose unemployment rate was higher than the national average and rising faster than the national average. The facade of the main building, which had not been altered since it was built in 1881, showed that it had housed the Mechanics' Institute, one of the antecedents of the polytechnic. However, the interior had been changed so many times that the original users would not have recognised it. The polytechnic also used other buildings including a former textile mill, parts of which had functioned, at various times during the previous hundred years, as a dance hall, a warehouse, a car showroom, a secondary school, a police station, and a chapel. This building was known by the students as 'The Slum'. Some of the windows were impossible to open and some were impossible to close. One of the polytechnic buildings was on the other side of a motorway. The buildings were kept clean, but they needed substantial maintenance. All of this was reminiscent of the polytechnic where I had studied.

My office was small, and it was the only one in the

Department of Economics that did not have a telephone. These two facts were not unrelated; the architect had intended the room to contain a toilet. The consolation was that I shared the office with only one other lecturer. The two desks were as far apart as possible, but they were almost touching each other. I could reach the door-handle, and open the door, without rising from my desk-chair.

The head of my department was welcoming and friendly on my first day in my new job, but he was obviously very busy, and he could not spend much time with me. I was given my timetable and shown the filing cabinet in the departmental office where syllabus documents were kept. There was no other briefing for newcomers. I was told to ask if I needed help.

An immediate difficulty was that all the drawers in my desk were locked and there was no key. I reported this and, the next day, a locksmith opened the drawers. They were full of empty whisky bottles. Nobody had told me that my predecessor was an alcoholic. Several of my new colleagues assured me that the stresses of the job did not always, or even frequently, lead to alcoholism.

My first lecture was on the second morning of my first week in the job. Most of the class, rows and rows of them, were there when I opened the door and stepped in, five minutes before the time I was due to start. Then my heart started racing and, since my right hand was still on the door-knob, I backed out and closed the door again. The corridor would surely be a good place to wait until my heart stopped leaping about. This tactic did not have the desired effect, so I opened the door and entered tentatively. The students laughed. One was laughing so much that he fell off his chair.

I stood at the table at the front of the room and waited for silence. A regiment of hot ants marched up my left cheek. I tried scratching, but it's difficult with wet fingers.

The laughing continued, so I asked for silence. Someone shouted some advice which I pretended not to hear, but the other students enjoyed it.

I looked at the audience and waited and waited. There were only thirty-five students in the class, but it looked like thirty-five hundred. Eventually, the laughter died away, so I picked up my notes and began the lecture. My handwriting was difficult to read because I could not hold the paper still. From time to time, I delivered one of the gestures that I had practised at the bathroom mirror the previous evening.

Suddenly, I reached the end of my notes. I looked at my watch and found that I had completed a one-hour lecture in thirty minutes. My progress had been more measured when I rehearsed the lecture in my flat. My heart moved into high gear again, and a pair of cockroaches did the Charleston between my shoulder blades.

I asked for questions. There were none. There was no option but to leave the room and close the door behind me. Unfortunately, the first door that I opened was a broom cupboard, but I got it right the second time and reached the sanctuary of the corridor. I then had to re-enter the classroom, to a crescendo of laughter, to retrieve my briefcase.

My first experience of lecturing was humiliating but my teaching (and public speaking) skills soon improved. I thought about the lecturers who had taught me, and I tried to learn from their successes and from their failures. I know that my teaching skills improved quickly because the students told me that this had happened. They congratulated me. They spoke to me as the confident and engaging lecturer that I had become, and they appeared to have forgotten the failure that I was. This included the students who had been present at my first lecture, which was a disaster. They were sympathetic perhaps partly because most of them had recovered from earlier failures to become undergraduate students of economics.

As I entered the building the morning after my first lecture, the head of my department greeted me. 'How did your first lecture go?'

I hesitated. 'Well, ...'

'Oh, that's good to hear. I knew you would settle in quickly. I knew you would do well in this job.' And he was off, briskly up the stairs to his office.

At the end of that week, he asked to see me. He said that he always talked to each inexperienced recruit about the need for ethical behaviour. He explained that a professional relationship must always be strictly dispassionate and unbiassed. He said that it is the same for doctors and their patients and for bank managers and applicants for large loans. He explained that I should never put myself in a position where it might look as if I might have taken a bribe. 'Just remember that you can be friendly, but the students are not your friends.' This advice seemed to me to be self-evident. I was surprised that it was stated explicitly, but I took it seriously.

Two months into my new job, one of my students invited me to a meal at his flat. Although he was two years older than me, he was a first-year student. The ethical guidelines I had been given told me to refuse this invitation. But I liked him, and I did not want to cause offence. In addition, I was alone in an unfamiliar city, and I needed a few friends.

I struggled with this issue. I knew that I should not do it, but after much tortuous thought, I decided to do it anyway. I consoled myself that this student was exceptionally capable and diligent and was certain to pass all his exams at the first attempt and with high marks, so there would never be any reason for anyone to accuse me of receiving a bribe. I accepted the invitation. But I knew

I had ignored good advice.

My student and his wife welcomed me and introduced me to their other guest. This was a single woman of about my age. I immediately felt a sensation that is difficult to describe. It was a combination of nausea and defiance. I decided instantaneously that I could not, and would not, allow one of my students to choose my next girlfriend. Suddenly, I regretted not taking ethical constraints more seriously.

Life does not always proceed in an orderly and predictable manner. It is almost fifty years since I married Claudia, whom I met at that meal (which I should not have attended). I hope that our annual celebration of the life-changing consequences of an unethical act is not unethical.

Most of the students at the polytechnic were on degree courses. Courses at lower levels, which were also interesting to teach, were being transferred to other institutions. Courses for University of London degrees had been replaced with courses validated by the Council for National Academic Awards.

The CNAA procedures were designed to be rigorous. Each proposal for a new degree course had to be described in a document that was hundreds of pages long. Detailed syllabuses were necessary but were not sufficient. The structure of the course, and of each of its parts, had to be described and justified. Assessment methods and details of the qualifications and experience of each of the lecturers had to be provided. Information on libraries, computers, and other amenities at the polytechnic was needed. Research activity was regarded by the CNAA as essential, so each submission document included details of lecturers' academic publications and current research.

Preparing documents for the CNAA was a time-consuming activity. There was often tension between the wish to produce a document that would be approved and the need to tell the whole truth. Many hours were spent in meetings discussing draft documents. I did not know about any of this when I applied for a job as a lecturer.

When, at last, I was again thinking clearly about my failed thesis, and partly because of the need to list my academic publications in documents submitted by the polytechnic to the CNAA, I decided to try to get some of my thesis published. Although I could now see major flaws in my thesis, I chose one of the core chapters and I added a lengthy introduction and a conclusion. I typed my article neatly, in the required format, and, as required, submitted three copies to the editor of an academic journal. The refereeing process took months, although it seemed longer. Eventually, without revisions being requested, my article was accepted. It was published in 1975. This was a cause for major celebration. The head of my department was pleased but, he said, not surprised. He said that he had always had confidence in me. As soon as my article was published, I sent a copy of it to my supervisor. In my letter, I expressed my thanks and sent good wishes. He did not reply.

The students' responses to my lectures were encouraging. They knew I had spent hours preparing the material that I presented, and they thanked me for this. Sometimes I prepared detailed notes for the students and distributed photocopies. I did this when the explanation of theory in the recommended textbook was unclear or to describe recent economic developments.

I wrote a commentary on the instruments of monetary policy that were introduced by the Bank of England in 1971, and a student said it was good enough to be published. I was not sure about this but, after revising it, I sent it to a major newspaper anyway. After a few days, it was accepted for publication, and it was in print the following week. The response was gratifying, and not only from within the polytechnic. One of the letters that I received was from the lecturer who, six years earlier, had described my first essay as 'rubbish'. He now wrote to congratulate me and to apologise for his brashness. He wrote 'You are an unlikely academic'.

My first year as a lecturer was exhilarating. I had found work that was interesting, enjoyable, and worthwhile. My colleagues were supportive and friendly. I also got on well with my students, perhaps partly because I was only a few years older than almost all of them. There were, of course, drawbacks to my new job. The most important was the number of hours that I had to work. In order to teach the classes that I was allocated, I worked until late every evening. Sometimes, I was only one lecture ahead of the students. A fund of prepared lecture notes takes considerable time to accumulate. And the other significant negative feature of my new job, which I had not predicted, was the large number of meetings that I had to attend. Sometimes, it seemed that meetings were more important than the activities and policies that were being discussed.

5
Meetings. Meetings. Meetings

When I began my first lecturing job, I did not predict the amount of time that I would spend in meetings, and I did not predict the effects that these meetings would have on my colleagues' (and probably my) behaviour.

Committees were a significant part of the constitutional arrangements at the polytechnic. Every course had a Course Committee, which consisted of relevant lecturers, their heads of department, student representatives, and others. Course Committees met at least once a term and made recommendations but not decisions. [In institutions running courses leading to CNAA degrees, a course was not a set of lectures and tutorials in a particular subject. It was a complete package of tuition and assessment in a large number of subjects, taking a minimum of three years for a full-time student to complete, leading to a qualification such as BA in Economics.]

A lecturer was asked to take minutes at each Course Committee meeting. The draft minutes were edited by the head of the department, who chaired these meetings, and then they were typed, re-edited, re-typed, photocopied, and distributed. Copies of minutes were sent to the principal of the polytechnic. Sometimes he wrote to the head of the department to express concern (which meant disapproval). Sometimes his concern referred to the literary style of the minutes. His memos were photocopied, distributed, and discussed at the next meeting. This discussion was minuted.

Each meeting of each Course Committee began with a discussion of the accuracy of the minutes of the previous meeting. Sometimes this part of the meeting was over in a few minutes but it frequently lasted thirty minutes or longer. I remember the chairman ruling that a person who was not present at a meeting was not entitled to comment on the accuracy of its minutes.

Proceedings of Course Committees were formal. Each person who contributed to the discussion began by saying 'Mr Chairman'. At the beginning of each meeting, the chairman addressed his introductory remarks to 'ladies and gentlemen'. When he had become weary of lengthy and repetitive and tedious (and perhaps acrimonious) discussion, he would say 'Can we make progress, gentlemen, please?' and he would always quickly add 'and ladies, of course'.

The agenda of each Course Committee meeting was distributed in advance. When important issues were to be discussed, some of my colleagues organised unofficial pre-meeting meetings, at which tactics would be planned. The chairman of the Course Committee was not invited to pre-meeting meetings but probably knew about them. Opposing groups held separate pre-meeting meetings. Sometimes, when the agreed tactics had not been followed, there would be post-meeting meetings, at which recriminations were assertively expressed.

Every course also had an Examinations Board, whose membership matched the Course Committee except for the student representatives. Examinations Boards met at the end of each exam season and made a decision on each candidate. In each subject, students who were not successful could be allowed to repeat the year of study, or not, at the discretion of the Examinations Board. External examiners were present at Examinations Board meetings, and all decisions were subject to their agreement. Most, but not all, external examiners took an active role. Marked exam scripts were sent to them before Examinations Board meetings. Sometimes, external examiners increased (or decreased) all exam marks by 5% or 10% or a similar figure. Sometimes they changed the marks of a few candidates. A small proportion of the external examiners never said anything and were described by some of my colleagues as brain-dead, but they received the same fees as those who participated fully.

In each department, there were meetings of the staff, including both academic and non-academic members. In the Department of Economics, these were conducted with the same formality as Course Committee meetings, but minutes were not photocopied and distributed. The head of the department assured us that these were informal gatherings, and not meetings, so minutes were not needed. After some of these meetings (or informal gatherings), each faction distributed its unofficial minutes, which were discussed at unofficial meetings to which the head of the department was not invited.

Even more time-consuming than the meetings of Course Committees were the meetings of Course Planning Committees. Their role was to prepare lengthy documents for submission to the CNAA. These documents were needed when the polytechnic proposed to introduce new courses or to revise existing courses. A chapter on research activity was needed in each submission. This was frequently seen as a problem. Although most of my colleagues had generated academic publications, some had not, and this was difficult to conceal. Despite this, the research record of each of my low-achieving colleagues was described in a generous (and often misleading) way.

Other meetings were less frequent and less socially

corrosive. Short-listed candidates for academic vacancies were interviewed. The process was formal and included lunch, at which the food was much more interesting than was usually available in the staff canteen. I was not invited to be a member of an interview panel until I had been a lecturer for several years. The first time this happened, the head of my department gave me a list of the questions he wanted me to ask each candidate. I said I would consider these suggestions but might decide to devise my own questions. Although my relationship with him became a little frosty at this point, it recovered quickly. He knew that he could not afford to have difficult relationships with a significant proportion of his colleagues at the same time.

Course proposals submitted to the CNAA were followed by a visit to the polytechnic by a team of experienced academics from universities and from other polytechnics. These visits were also formally structured and included impressive lunches. The meetings included discussions with senior and junior academic staff. The week before each CNAA visit, there was a rehearsal, known as a mock visit. There were harsh words for those lecturers who did not take this seriously. When a visit did not proceed smoothly, there would be a post-visit meeting, known as a *post-mortem*. Nobody enjoyed these. Some of my colleagues were not happy that CNAA visiting panels included academics from other polytechnics (which offered similar courses and competed for the same students). They wondered whether there might be significant conflicts of interest that could influence the visiting panel's decisions. This seemed to me to be unlikely.

Meetings of the Appeals Board were formal in a different way. Most of the members of the Appeals Board were lecturers at the polytechnic. Although nobody knew why, the Appeals Board included a nominee of the local city council. This person was usually not an academic. Students who appealed against a decision of an Examinations Board had to attend a quasi-judicial hearing, at which they could present their case and submit evidence. The chairman of the Examinations Board defended its decisions. Lecturers could be summoned and cross-examined. I received a summons only once. The hearing was interesting, and I am confident that the correct decision was reached. I am equally confident that the city-council representative had had little education and did not understand some of the issues. The day before the hearing, the head of my department said that he was not going to give me any guidance about what I should say. He said he had confidence in my good judgement. He then gave me detailed suggestions. Fortunately, not many students submitted appeals and these hearings were infrequent.

Occasionally, an *ad hoc* committee of senior people, usually accompanied by a small number of younger lecturers, would be appointed to consider an important issue. Like all meetings, these *ad hoc* committees were formal. Minutes were prepared, typed, edited, typed, re-edited, re-typed, photocopied, and distributed. These minutes were discussed in other committees and these discussions were recorded in the minutes of these committees. A recurrent issue was the encouragement of research activity and especially the encouragement of research achievement in the form of academic publications. This was a difficult problem to address because the causes of low (or zero) achievement were beyond the control of anyone in the polytechnic. Many of the low achievers had been appointed before there were undergraduate courses at this institution, and the selection processes, when they had applied for their lecturing jobs, had not referred to their (lack of) academic publications. At their interviews, they had not been asked about their research achievements.

In addition, the long hours and the crowded conditions, including multiple occupation of small offices, were not conducive to original work. It is perhaps remarkable how many, not how few, of the lecturers had achieved a significant number of academic publications.

The intentions of the committee system were undoubtedly good. Its effects, however, were not always desirable. The large number of (often protracted) meetings crowded out more productive activity. Resources were diverted from teaching and research into organising meetings, devising and distributing agendas, preparing for meetings (including attending pre-meeting meetings), attending meetings, writing and distributing minutes, discussing the minutes, and recording and commenting on these discussions. This had a corrupting effect on behaviour. For some of my colleagues, scoring points at meetings became more important than the issues being discussed. There was often tension between honour and expediency. For example, when preparing a submission to the CNAA, it was usually seen as more important to describe the research activity at the polytechnic in a favourable way than to tell the whole truth. However, for some of my colleagues, it was a moral imperative, regardless of the consequences, to be brutally honest. Senior people felt under considerable pressure not to be the identifiable cause of a rejection by the CNAA of an undergraduate course proposal.

As he tried to maintain a semblance of dignity in a difficult situation that he could not control, the head of my department made me think of a piece of driftwood being thrown by waves against a rocky shore and then righting itself on the water before being dragged out to sea again and then, once again, being thrown onto the rocks and then righting itself on the water ....

It is possible that the changes in attitudes and

behaviour that were caused by excessive use of meetings also afflicted the people on CNAA visiting panels. One of my colleagues wrote a satirical definition. 'A review by the CNAA is an opportunity for those who know the truth and wish to conceal it to give misleading answers in response to irrelevant questions asked by those who suspect the truth and wish to avoid hearing it.' However, my belief was that this summary was much too cynical (but unfortunately not in every case).

Everyone knew that this situation was absurd, but no-one knew how to stop it. Whatever issue was being discussed, nobody wanted to let the other side win. Many of my colleagues felt that they were in too weak a position to be assertive. The principal of the polytechnic and many of his immediate colleagues had become so mesmerised by administrative procedures and precedents, by the need to keep detailed records, and by the consequences of failure, that they might have lost real contact with teaching and with academic research. Nobody wanted to admit that the emperor was wearing no clothes.

6
First Conference Presentation

Four years after becoming a lecturer, I presented my first paper at an academic conference. A lecturer in computing at the same polytechnic had taught me about computer modelling and, after months of work together, we wrote an article on the results of simulating an economic model, which I had devised, and which had been published in an academic journal. We were able to predict the immediate and delayed effects of certain shocks to several versions of a simple economic and political system. On behalf of us both, I presented these results at a conference on modelling and simulation. The conference proceedings were published as a book about a year later.

Contributions to the conference were invited six months in advance. Our paper was almost complete, so we submitted a proposal. It was more than five months before we were informed that our paper had been accepted.

It took me several hours to drive to the polytechnic where the conference was held. I had received a copy of the conference programme two days before it began, but I did not read it until I was in my hotel bedroom the evening before the opening session. I was disappointed that, unlike most of the material to be presented, my paper was not summarised. It was listed with nine others under the heading 'Other Contributed Papers'. I was to give my lecture during the afternoon of the second (and last) day of the conference, which was a disappointment. Much more worrying, however, was that the titles of most of the other papers meant little to me (and the titles of the remaining papers meant nothing to me). They dealt, as I should have expected, with simulation theory and methods rather than with the results of applying simulation methods to particular models. The small number of applied papers referred to laboratory sciences and to engineering and not to economic issues. I was immediately worried about the questions at the end of my talk. I was worried that I would be unable to answer them (or even to understand them).

This was the first academic conference to be run at this polytechnic, and it showed. There were fifty participants at the conference, and it was held in a room with forty seats. The first welcoming speech, by the principal of the polytechnic, was delayed by ten minutes while more chairs were brought in and placed along a wall. These were stacking chairs with moulded plastic seats. I found that their shape did not match the shape of my body. Within fifteen minutes, I had backache. Not long after, I felt that I might be developing bedsores.

The welcoming speeches did not take longer than an hour, and then the specialist lectures began. My fears were justified; the first lecture was incomprehensible to me. The second and the third were too. By lunchtime, I felt punch-drunk. I had been immersed by an impenetrable alien culture.

Most of the lecturers had prepared slides to illustrate their talks but these, far from helping, made things worse for me. PowerPoint had not yet been invented, so these slides were handwritten, which meant that some of them were difficult (or impossible) to read. To be shown a closely-packed page of hand-written algebra, splattered with Greek characters, meant little, especially if there was insufficient time to read it before it was replaced with another similar page.

During the afternoon, I gave up trying to follow the lectures and only my plastic chair kept me awake.

From the afternoon, it was obvious that the audience was becoming restless, and I gained some comfort from this. I hoped this meant that other people were as baffled as I was, but I knew that it might have been due to the lack of ventilation or to the uncomfortable seating. It might even have indicated that the lectures were too elementary, but I tried strenuously to ignore this possibility.

When it was my turn to speak, I mounted the platform, stood at the lectern and, unlike the other speakers, waited for silence. I always waited for silence before starting a lecture.

'Do make a start, Mr Mushin', said the conference chairman, after less than two minutes had elapsed.

'I'm waiting for silence,' I said.

'Ah, yes', said the chairman, looking uneasy.

Eventually, the talkers stopped talking and their neighbours stopped nudging them, and I began the lecture. To my intense surprise, all members of the audience listened. Many were taking notes. Later that afternoon, after the formal part of the conference ended, I was told by several members of the audience that my lecture was the first interesting one at the conference.

At the end of my lecture, the chairman invited questions. A man at the back of the room stood up and started speaking. This was a lengthy question, perhaps verging on a lecture in itself. It lasted for several minutes and then, after a pause, he started speaking again. I quickly lost the thread of what the man was saying, but I was encouraged that the chairman looked puzzled.

Suddenly, without making it clear whether an answer was expected, the questioner sat down.

There was a silence. The chairman looked at me.

'Mr Mushin?'

I was determined to reply without hesitating. 'Yes, indeed, this is a most interesting contribution. I have a lot of sympathy with your point of view, but I am not sure that this conference platform is the most appropriate place to discuss these issues. I prefer to deal with matters of elucidation at this point and to leave the discussion of the wider implications of my work until after the conference proceedings have ended.'

'I entirely agree', said the chairman with a smile.

After the tenth of the 'Other Contributed Papers', the chairman presented his closing address. Then people stood up and drifted, chatting, out of the room. There were a lot of encouraging comments on my paper, which, of course, I enjoyed hearing. I was approached by a man who looked familiar. I did not know who he was. Suddenly, I understood. He was the professor who had supervised the writing of my thesis, which was subsequently judged to be a failure, when I was a Research Assistant.

'Congratulations, very well done', he said warmly. 'I really liked your paper. It's basically a tedious topic, as I'm sure you will agree, but you almost made it come alive. By leaving out the mathematical jargon and concentrating on the economic effects, you made it into the only worthwhile item in the whole conference. Yes, absolutely. Well done. I did not know that you had such a flair for public speaking. I was not expecting you to be good at academic work.'

I was amused that I had, again, been identified as an unlikely academic.

'Thank you for those generous comments', I said. I did not explain that the mathematics that I had omitted was not only boring, but it was also, to me, impossible to understand.

'Now', continued the professor, 'I have a proposition to put to you. I'm the founding editor of a new journal of applied economics. Can I include your paper in the first issue?'

I was taken by surprise. 'I would be delighted, of course,' I said, 'but there will be copyright matters to be sorted out. The proceedings of this conference are going to be published as a book, so you will need the agreement of the publisher.'

'Damn,' said the professor.

7
Information Evening

I attended my first Information Evening about six months after I became a lecturer. This event, which was held each year at a secondary school, was intended to provide information to sixth-formers (and often their parents) about employment opportunities and tertiary education in the region. Major employers and educational institutions were represented. A lecturer from each department at the polytechnic was asked to be present. Although the polytechnic, and each department within it, wanted to increase its enrolment of students, these events in the 1970s were not comparable to the intense marketing activities that became commonplace in universities and other institutions a generation later.

I returned to my office after a lecture to find a note stuck to the door with an inch of Sellotape. The message, underlined in red, was 'Please see me urgently'. Although there was no signature, I knew the handwriting. The head of my department always communicated in this way. I postponed the cup of coffee that I needed and went to his office.

'Have you any plans for tomorrow evening?' he asked. This question seemed intrusive, so I hesitated before replying.

'That's good', he said, assuming an answer despite having allowed barely enough time for one. 'What I want you to do is this. There's an Information Evening tomorrow at 7.30 and I want you to be our department's representative. Is that OK?'

'It's very short notice,' I said tentatively.

'Yes, I know. And I'm sorry. The memo about this reached me this morning. It's dated two weeks ago, but I received it this morning. I'm asking you because you don't have a wife or children, so it's easier for you to take these things on than it is for other lecturers.'

I disliked his style, so I made a token protest. 'I don't think my domestic arrangements should affect the way that I am treated by my employer.'

'Of course. Of course. No question of that, of course. You're absolutely right. I'm asking you because you are a man of integrity and of good judgement. I'm sure that you are the best man for this important job. I know I can rely on you to do it well.' His writhing posture showed that I had embarrassed him, but I could see no point in turning this minor skirmish into a war.

'Yes, I'll do it'.

'Good. Thank you. Please remember what is expected of you. We need to find more students for the BA in Economics course. Any students with any interest in the subject should be encouraged to follow it up. And do be positive about the facilities at the polytechnic.'

'I shall not tell any lies.'

'No, no, of course not. Certainly not. I am not asking you to do that. But please be selective about the truths that you tell.'

The Information Evening was held at one of the secondary schools in the city. It was a prominent stone building. A diamond-shaped panel above the main entrance said 'AD 1882'. I carried an apple-box of pamphlets up the steps, and I was handed a list of the Visiting Consultants and the rooms to which they had been allocated.

In the classroom to which I had been sent, some of the desks might have dated from the foundation of the school. I arranged the pamphlets in neat piles, pinned a colourful poster ('A Choice of Opportunities and the Opportunity of Your Choice') over a crudely-drawn map of Australia on the blackboard, pulled the front row of chairs closer and sat at the teacher's desk. The poster included carefully-posed photographs of students listening to a lecturer, in a laboratory, in the library, and enjoying a Saturday dance. The students did not look relaxed.

It was a busy evening. With a few exceptions, my conversations with sixth-formers and their parents were interesting and useful. Most of the prospective students had clear ideas about what they wanted to do and had already found out what courses were available and where. My guess is that most (or even all) of the people in the greatest need of help and guidance were not at the Information Evening. My memories of this event are mostly about the minority of parents who were misinformed about tertiary education or who excluded their children from their discussions with me. Some families continued to fight old battles in my presence.

'My daughter wants to do an economics degree.'

'No, I don't. I want to do a sociology degree.'

'I've told you again and again. And your mother agrees with me. There's no future in that kind of degree.'

'You don't know that. What sort of work do graduates in sociology do?'

'Nothing that you want to do.'

'You're mixing up sociology with social work.'

'No, I'm not.'

'Yes, you are. And what's wrong with social work, anyway?'

I coughed to remind them of my presence, but it was not loud enough to have any effect. I coughed again, louder, and father and daughter looked at me. The daughter spoke to me.

'Does your college do degrees in sociology?'

'We have degree courses in economics, in accountancy, and in business studies, and each of these includes sociology as a minor subject.'

'That sounds interesting', said her father.

'No, it doesn't. I want to do a specialist degree in sociology.'

There were other people waiting to see me so I said, 'I suggest that you should take one of each of these pamphlets and go and think about what questions you want to ask me.' They took the pamphlets and left the room. They did not return.

Some parents had not understood the requirements for admission to undergraduate courses.

'My son will probably fail his exams. Will that be a problem?' His son's response, behind his father's back, was to poke out his tongue. His father did not know why I smiled, which I could not stop myself doing. After a pause, he continued. 'Do you take that sort of thing seriously?'

'Yes, of course we do. The entry requirements for our degree courses are the same as at other polytechnics and at universities.'

'You don't mean that, do you?'

'Yes, I do'.

As I left the building, at the end of the evening, I congratulated myself that I had kept my promise to the head of my department. I had consistently told the truth. The next morning, he asked me how things went.

'It was an interesting evening.' I was nervous about saying anything that I would regret.

'But did you recruit any students for next year?'

'It's difficult to say. There's nothing definite, of course, but we'll probably get an increase in applications.'

This meaningless statement was taken at face value, but perhaps the head of my department knew what it really meant.

'Good. Good. Well done. Very well done. I knew I had chosen the right man for this job.'

In the 1970s and the early 1980s, I attended a large number of Information Evenings, and I always found them to be interesting. They were probably useful for the prospective students that I saw. For me, the most interesting people at each of these occasions were the parents who were misguided or who ignored their children during their discussions with me. A small number of parents showed no interest in what their children wanted to do or even in what they said. Some parents thought they could bully their children into becoming undergraduate students. Some of the potential students regarded their parents with contempt and I could see why.

Educational institutions' behaviour has evolved rapidly, and this has been particularly evident in their efforts to increase their student numbers. Pamphlets and posters have become larger and more colourful. They have included an increasing amount of irrelevant information (which is often misleading). Cartoons and other gimmicks have often been inserted into pamphlets on almost every page. The emphasis has moved away from information towards marketing and persuasion. Promotional events in the polytechnic buildings have included lectures, live music, films, and laboratory demonstrations. Specialist staff have been employed to run recruitment campaigns. Large advertisements, which are frequently misleading, have appeared in newspapers.

However, this intensification of recruitment (and marketing) activity has not had any obvious benefits. It has been impossible to prove that students (or their parents) have been attracted to institutions that have presented themselves in this way. Although there has been no evidence that expensive advertising has changed the behaviour of anyone, it is certain that my students, and their lecturers, have been irritated by it.

8
Experienced Lecturer

I quickly realised that I had found work that suited me. I became more efficient at preparing for lectures and more confident in delivering them. I enjoyed the students' responses to my lectures and tutorials, which was always encouraging. Meetings were often a time-consuming nuisance, of course, but I tried to devote no more than the minimum attention to them.

I got on well with my students. These relationships were less formal than I recall with my lecturers when I was a student. This was probably partly because almost all of my lecturers were more than twice my age and a significant proportion of them were more than three times my age. In marked contrast, I was the same generation as my students.

I remember a tutorial at which I had explained a complex piece of theory. During my explanation I wrote several lines of algebra on the blackboard. Before moving on to the next topic, I checked that every member of the class had understood the mathematics. One of the students was hesitant, so I said I would explain again. 'Watch the board and I'll run through it.'

Everyone laughed. I couldn't understand why, so I said it again. 'Watch the board and I'll run through it.' There was more laughter. Then, suddenly, I understood, and I joined in the laughter.

In the corridor after the tutorial, one of my students

said 'You could be a comedian. I like your style. It was absolutely convincing that you didn't know why we were laughing'.

Occasionally, I was offered part-time work by external bodies. For a year, I taught a weekly class of eight prisoners at a high-security prison. They took their studies seriously, and so did I, and we also had a few laughs together. This teaching was at secondary-school level, and there were no exams. It was partly as a reward for good behaviour that these prisoners were allowed to attend my classes. This was worthwhile work, and I enjoyed it, but I found the prison environment oppressive. I especially did not like being searched as I entered the prison and searched again when I left.

I became a part-time tutor for The Open University, which was then a new and experimental institution. I had a mixed reaction to this work. Most of the students were capable of undergraduate study and worked hard at it. However, there were also students who had been misled by deceptive advertising and who were not equipped with the skills that they needed. Some did not have a sufficient level of literacy. These students did not pass (or, usually, even attend) their exams. Most of them were deeply resentful that they had wasted their money and their time.

I also lectured at the nearest police training college. My class consisted of twenty-five sergeants who were likely to be further promoted. This was a committed and enthusiastic group of students, and I enjoyed teaching them. However, I found the formalities of the college to be unfamiliar (and a little strange). Everyone was in uniform, and all tunics were fully buttoned at all times (even on the warmest days). Male hair was short and female hair was short or in a tight bun. Senior officers (and part-time lecturers) were addressed as 'sir' or 'ma'am'. The classroom had about thirty seats and was tiered. As I entered the room, accompanied by a senior officer, before starting each lecture, all the sergeants stood. They remained standing (and still) until I invited them to sit. Before each of the lunches to which I was invited every time I taught at the college, hundreds of cadets, officers, and senior officers stood in silence while grace was said.

When I was informed that my thesis was a failure, I felt that I had achieved nothing while I was working as a Research Assistant. However, it gradually became clear to me that I had acquired valuable experience, knowledge, and skills. I had learnt about the use of statistical methods in economic research. I knew how to obtain economic data and how to draw interesting and valid conclusions from it, and I was able to apply this to my own original work and in partnership with colleagues who did not have my computer experience. The technology had quickly changed, and I no longer had to use paper tape to input data, but the principles that I had learnt were of lasting value.

My first article in an academic journal was almost identical to a chapter of my (failed) thesis. I then wrote academic articles on unrelated research topics that were also published. This was satisfying, and it pleased senior colleagues who included the details in CNAA submission documents. All of this was encouraging, but my main interest remained in my teaching work.

Visits from publishers' representatives were irregular, sometimes frequent, and always unannounced. Although it was useful to hear about new textbooks, almost all of these salespeople knew little (or nothing) about the subjects that these books are intended to teach. They usually compensated by showing intense enthusiasm and *bonhomie*, for which they probably had powerful financial incentives.

An extreme case was the man who told me, 'We're a

dynamic American publisher of academic texts. We are a major player in the market for university textbooks in all fifty states. And we are expanding into the British market. Our office in Australia is very successful, so we'll do well here. The Australians are nearly as British as the British, aren't they?' He laughed loudly but, seeing my expressionless face, stopped abruptly.

The evolution of the polytechnic where I worked was rapid enough to be obvious. The average level of academic ability of each cohort of students declined and, more importantly, so did the average level of their commitment to undergraduate study. It is difficult to be certain about the causes of this. However, among them was probably the expansion of the universities, which nobody had ever believed had had the 'parity of esteem' with the polytechnics that the Ministry of Education described. This had led to fewer capable applicants for places on degree courses at polytechnics. Rising unemployment, especially among eighteen-year-olds, was also likely to be relevant. Many of the uncommitted students probably wanted a job and chose full-time study because it was better than being unemployed. They might also have believed (or hoped) that possession of a degree would impress employers. Whatever the causes, the outcome was that there was a large and noticeable minority of students who should not have been attempting undergraduate courses. These students constituted a kind of human sludge in the system. They became demoralised and this affected the other students (and their lecturers). Many of these weak students failed (or did not attend) their first-year exams, so failure rates increased. Among my colleagues, this caused an increasing fear of closure of departments, or even of the whole institution, especially as Margaret Thatcher's government was determined to make severe cuts in government expenditure. This made the effects of the meetings malaise (or mania) even more serious.

About five years after I started work as a lecturer, I began applying for advertised jobs again. I was ready for a change, and I was tired of the pervasive effects of meetings. I was interviewed, but not appointed, at several universities. As a result of cuts in government spending, the academic labour market was very competitive. In various ways, I was told, each time, that I would have been chosen if there had not been a better candidate. At one of my university interviews, I was told that more than one hundred applications had been received and that only six candidates were being interviewed. This was not a great consolation.

My applications to polytechnics were more successful. Most led to interviews, and I was successful at several of these. However, I did not accept any of these offers of employment. Each of the polytechnics that I visited was under-resourced and over-crowded. These were familiar issues. Chatting to members of the interview panel over (an always lavish) lunch revealed that each institution had the same entrenched system of committees, producing the same social responses and frictions from which I wanted to escape. It was not worth the upheaval of moving to another city to find that nothing in my work had improved.

The interviews at polytechnics were interesting. Some of the interviewers revealed more than they intended. I asked an interviewer about the content of the BA in Combined Studies course that he had told me proudly was in an advanced stage of planning. I asked him to define 'Combined Studies'. He congratulated me on asking a pertinent question. Then, with some embarrassment, he admitted that he did not know anything about the proposed course. The name of the course had occurred to him only that morning.

A friend of mine, who had been a lecturer at the same polytechnic, accepted an offer of a job at a university in New Zealand. He wrote to me full of enthusiasm for his new country. The job was interesting, the people were kind, the salary was generous, and the climate was magnificent. 'It's late autumn here, but it's hotter than the hottest summer that I can remember.' For the first time, I considered applying for overseas jobs.

I applied for lecturing jobs in economics that were advertised by New Zealand universities. I was short-listed for none of these vacancies, which was not encouraging. Then I saw an advertisement in *The Economist* that was inserted by an economic research and consultancy institute in New Zealand. They were looking for a graduate in economics who had a record of academic publications. I was hesitant about applying because I did not want to give up lecturing, but Claudia encouraged me to submit an application. 'You don't want to be in the same job until you retire, or until you die, which will probably be sooner if you don't find a new employer quickly.' There is always something inspiring about Claudia when she is being assertive. I decided that the job looked interesting, and that I had nothing to lose, so I submitted the completed form, a *curriculum vitae*, and photocopies of some of my articles. I was not expecting to be interviewed.

I was invited to meet the chief executive of the institute who would be in London to interview the short-listed candidates. I was apprehensive, but I had no reason to be. This interview was without stress. More than that, it was enjoyable. It was a sunny day (although probably not warm by New Zealand standards) and we sat on a park bench and watched people feeding the birds. We discussed all aspects of the advertised job and lots of other things. We had lunch together in a café and then sat on a bench in another park. By the end of the day, my interviewer probably knew almost as much about me as I did, but his questions were not intrusive. This conversation taught me how little I knew about New Zealand. For example, although I knew that the New Zealand government that was elected in 1984 was following Thatcherite policies, I had not understood how extreme some of these were.

Some weeks later, I was offered the post of Senior Economist. This was, of course, subject to obtaining immigrant visas for Claudia and me and for Stephen, our son. After initial doubts, we decided to ignore our emotional turmoil, and I accepted the contract. This was a difficult decision. I would be giving up lecturing, which I enjoyed, and taking on a new type of work. We would be abandoning friends and familiar places. As usual, Claudia gave me good advice. 'What was the point of going all the way to London to be interviewed if you're not going to take the job?'

It took months to get the visas. It seemed like years, but it was only a few months. As soon as they arrived, I resigned from my job. The head of my department said he had enjoyed working with me, which had not always been true. Claudia resigned from her teaching job, and she wrote to several possible employers in New Zealand. We put a For Sale sign on our house, and asked friends if they would like to buy our car. Stephen, who was then seven years old, was initially unenthusiastic about emigrating, but fairly quickly got used to the idea.

We spent a lot of time looking at books about New Zealand and we asked each other questions. Claudia asked me, 'Will we be living on the coast or inland? Is the area flat or hilly? Agricultural or mining or neither?' I didn't know any of the answers, so Claudia had won, but she hadn't really won because she didn't know the answers either. We laughed a lot, and we might have learnt something about New Zealand. Stephen joined in the fun.

For him, it appeared to be evidence of parental insanity. The three of us were embarking on an uncertain but exciting adventure.

9
A New Country

I started work in New Zealand in January 1986. At the research institute where I was employed, I was not involved in contract research for clients. I was assigned to the group that prepared regular forecasts of the New Zealand macroeconomy. I had experience of research in macroeconomics, and I had taught specialised undergraduate courses in this area. I was able to participate in this work. I had the right skills to analyse data, and I was able to prepare written material for publication. I contributed to seminars on the latest predictions. My colleagues were friendly and very supportive to newcomers.

Although my role at the institute was not beyond my abilities, and I worked hard at it, it did not hold my attention as much as I hoped it would. It quickly reminded me that I was principally a teacher. I missed having regular contact with students. I particularly missed helping weaker students to master complex theory. I had been such a student, and I have not forgotten the help that I received from my lecturers. Some of my colleagues were part-time tutors at the university in the city, so I telephoned the lecturer who was in charge of the first-year course in economics. I introduced myself and asked about vacancies for tutors.

'I have one question for you,' he said. 'Do you have a degree in economics?'

'Yes,' I replied.

'Then you have got the job. Congratulations. I'll arrange to have you sent a part-time employment contract'.

The speed of this negotiation was startling. It took less than two minutes. I was expecting to be interviewed. I later learnt that there were a large number of vacancies for tutors and no applicants.

I agreed to take two tutorial groups per week. At the start of the new academic year, when my tutorials began, I felt as though I was coming home. This was the best kind of work for me. This was where I belonged. I found that the most rewarding part of each working week was the morning that I was at the university.

I knew how to run tutorials because I had been doing it for many years, but my new role was not the same as my previous job. There were about nine hundred students on the first-year course in economics. The biggest lecture theatre had 340 seats, so there were three lecture streams, which were taught by different lecturers. There were about seventy-five tutorial groups, and most of the tutors were part-time. I was not used to such a large-scale operation. This was not the kind of course that I had taught in my previous job, where the classes were small, and I knew every student. The students in my tutorial groups at the university joked that the course was run like an industry (and it was a major employer). The effect of this was that I knew neither the lecturers nor the other tutors. The students did not know their lecturers and *vice versa*. Each student knew only a tiny proportion of the other students on the same course. All of this was new to me.

After a few months, I was invited to give some lectures on a specialised course at the university. Some of my academic publications were related to this topic. It was good to be asked, and I enjoyed this work too.

Claudia and I were rapidly at ease in our new country.

The common language, and the largely common culture, made it easy for us. From the UK, New Zealand must be one of the easiest countries to move to. Claudia's qualifications were recognised, and she found suitable work without difficulty. Stephen liked his primary school. He wanted to sound like the other children and strenuously tried to acquire a Kiwi accent. He joined a soccer team (which was not available for seven-year-olds in the suburb where we lived in the UK) and, although he had never been part of an organised team before, scored a goal in his first match. Migrating to New Zealand was a gamble, of course, but it was the best decision. All three of us had won.

One of the things that Claudia and I did not know until we arrived was that there are frequent earthquakes in New Zealand. In most cases, these cause very little damage, but they can be very serious. Like most people, I always find earthquakes unsettling. They are impossible to predict, which compounds the emotional effects. The climate was an unexpected bonus. The Mediterranean summers were very welcome.

Although it did not take me long to feel at home in New Zealand, it was many months (or, probably, longer) before I acquired the general knowledge that the locals had. I listened to weather forecasts on the radio, but I did not know whether the places that were mentioned were at the other end of the country or within walking distance. I had not heard of recent noteworthy politicians. About a month after I started work at the institute, a senior colleague asked me to visit a prominent entrepreneur the following week. He told me the location of the office that I was to visit. I asked whether I would need to book a flight. This produced laughter because the office was only a fifteen-minute drive away. I frequently felt uneducated in my first few months in New Zealand. I tried doggedly to overcome this, and I probably succeeded (most of the time).

Macroeconomic research in New Zealand in the late 1980s was undertaken in the context of the restructuring of the economy that was introduced by the government that won the 1984 election. There was extensive deregulation of the private sector, sale of state assets, cuts in government expenditure, and changes to the tax system. A frequent slogan was 'User pays'. The objectives included greater efficiency, more powerful incentives, increased competition, more choice for consumers, decreased government debt, and reduced inflation. The immediate consequences included increased unemployment and increased inequality. This suite of policies became known as 'Rogernomics', after Roger Douglas, the Minister of Finance.

A very tight monetary policy was one of the features of Rogernomics. Claudia and I experienced its effects directly when we sought a loan to buy a house. The bank official told us that the interest rate would be 21.5%. I thought he was trying to be funny. I had not previously encountered such a high interest rate on a house-purchase loan.

Among my colleagues at the institute, opinions on Rogernomics were divided. I was uneasy about the probable effects of the new approach to running the economy. This was partly because, from 1979, I had seen the effects of Margaret Thatcher's policies on the declining industrial city where I lived. These included an unemployment rate, especially among school-leavers, which increased at an accelerating rate. Some of my colleagues were, however, strong supporters of the new approach.

My job did not just consist of analysing data. I was also required to meet important people in government departments, the Reserve Bank of New Zealand, large companies, and other bodies. I would not have had the opportunity to meet such people if I had not accepted the job in New Zealand. I was invited to meet the Minister of Finance at his office in the parliament building. Especially at a time of major economic and political controversies related to Rogernomics, this was an important opportunity. Until I came to New Zealand, I had not considered that I would ever be able to have a lengthy conversation with a prominent (and controversial) politician. For all of these reasons, my new job was a significant part of my education.

Each set of published economic forecasts that was prepared by the team of which I was a member was discussed on Radio New Zealand, and I was interviewed several times. This was another new experience. My contributions to these conversations must have been useful because Radio New Zealand invited me back to explain and discuss the background to other current economic issues that were not directly related to my work at the institute. These radio conversations were also part of my education.

When the university where I was tutoring (and occasionally lecturing) advertised a vacancy for a Lecturer in Economics, I saw this as an opportunity that I was determined not to miss. It was only a little more than a year since this university had not short-listed me for a similar vacancy, but I tried to forget this. I submitted a detailed application, with copies of academic publications, a *curriculum vitae*, and the completed application form. I was hoping for an interview, but not seriously expecting that this would happen. To my great surprise and delight, I was offered the job, to begin at the start of the next academic year.

The strange thing about this new appointment was that there was no interview. I was living in the same city as my prospective employer, which made it even stranger. Perhaps my tutoring and occasional lecturing were seen as a probationary period in which I had been successful. Perhaps my references from senior colleagues at the institute where I was working had been so glowing that an interview was not needed, but this seemed not only unlikely but absurd. Whatever the explanation, I was mystified, but this did not interfere with my elation at the good news. I had found my way back into the kind of job that I liked doing and that I had proved that I was good at.

I worked at the institute for one year. It was good experience, and I learnt a lot, but it was not the job for me. However, some of my ex-colleagues remain friends. These include the former chief executive of the institute, whom I met in London. His decision to offer me a job brought Claudia and me, and our son, to New Zealand. This improved our lives enormously. All three of us will always be grateful for that.

10
Lecturing again

The head of the Department of Economics showed me around on my first morning as a lecturer. He apologised for the size of my office. He explained that the two rows of prefabs that included my office were about to be replaced with much grander accommodation. I saw no reason for his apology. I had been allocated a room to myself and it was several times the size of the shared office that I used the last time that I was a lecturer.

He asked tentatively how I felt about teaching large classes. 'Some members of the department find them an almost impossible burden,' he said. I assured him that I would be happy to teach large classes. At that moment, I was thinking of my last lecturing job, where the largest class had about thirty-five students. Then I remembered that first-year lectures had 340 students, but I tried not to think about this.

By the next day, I was getting worried about large lectures. I had never done this kind of teaching. I worried whether my voice would be heard, especially at the back of the room. I relaxed a bit when one of my colleagues told me, 'There's a microphone you can use, so they'll always be able to hear you in the back row'.

At the lecture theatre where I was to give my first lecture, all of the 340 seats were taken. The rows of seats were steeply raked and curved in a semi-circle so that, at any time, I could not look at more than a small proportion of the students. There was no microphone. There were two cupboards. The first contained an empty Coca-Cola bottle and a mouldy half-eaten sandwich. The second was locked. I had looked in all the obvious places, but there was no microphone. I pretended not to notice this, and I began the lecture. To my great relief, even the students at the back were attentive and they took notes, so they must have been able to hear me. I was unsure about this, so I paused after fifteen minutes and I asked the class, 'Am I speaking loudly enough? Can you hear me clearly?' A student in the fourth row stood up, cupped his left hand behind his ear in an exaggerated mime of deafness, and said 'You what?' Everyone laughed. 'Don't listen to Groucho,' said someone near the back, 'we'll be able to hear you. There's no echo in this room.'

As I was gathering up my papers at the end of my first lecture, Groucho greeted me. 'That was awesome', he said. 'It was much better than the two lectures I went to this morning.'

'What was wrong with them?'

'Don't ask,' he replied with feeling.

I discovered the next morning that microphones in lecture theatres needed to be ordered two days in advance but, by then, I knew that I did not need one.

About a month later, the head of my department asked me to be the co-ordinator of the first-year course. This role included the appointment, training, and supervision of the part-time tutors. This sounded like an onerous task, and I really did not want it, but I did not protest. As the co-ordinator of a course with nine hundred students, I would be allocated fewer teaching hours. Although this confirmed that the role would be demanding, it was also a disappointment because teaching was what I wanted to spend my time doing.

I decided that my first task as course co-ordinator

would be to meet the part-time tutors, so I called a meeting. There was no e-mail in 1987, so I left telephone messages. The meeting was attended by about fifteen tutors, which was a small proportion of them. I asked them to introduce themselves to the meeting.

'I have been tutoring since I retired from schoolteaching. Since there are usually no spare seats at my classes, it looks like the students enjoy them. I do too. And I don't have to deal with crowd control, deliberate rudeness, smoking in the toilets, lost sports shoes, obnoxious parents, etc.'

'I'm a postgraduate. Progress on my thesis is incredibly slow, so I shall probably be a tutor on this course for years and years. I usually enjoy tutoring. But note the qualifier in that sentence.'

'I was unemployed for three years, which was not much fun. Neither is tutoring, of course, but it is better than being unemployed. I'm not very interested in economics, but that's the degree that I have got, so that's what I have got to teach. I hope to get out of teaching soon.'

This meeting was the first time that these tutors had met each other. They exchanged telephone numbers and, at the end of the meeting, when I left to go to my next lecture, they continued talking earnestly. This reminded me that there are likely to be communications problems within an organisation as complex and unwieldy as a course with nine hundred students. I was again reminded of this a few days after tutors had returned the assignments that they had marked to their authors.

A student came to see me. 'I have two friends,' he said, and paused. I waited. This was not a promising beginning.

'I have two friends,' he said again. There was another pause, and then the rest of the paragraph rushed out at me. 'And these two friends wrote equally good essays and, although I'm only a first-year student, I know these essays are equally good because I did this subject in the sixth form and I got an *A*, but they were marked by different tutors and one failed and the other passed. This is obviously unfair, especially as essay marks are part of the course assessment. There's a lot of this sort of thing happening in this course. And what are you going to do about it?'

I hesitated before replying. Although it was obvious that he was genuinely feeling aggrieved, it was not clear to me who was being accused and of what, especially as I had not been told the identity of the tutors, of the essay writers, or even of the complainant himself. If he was claiming that a tutor had shown favouritism, then I would pursue this matter strenuously. If, however, his sense of injustice arose because he had allowed a friend to copy his essay, and then found that the plagiarist's essay was awarded a pass and his essay a fail, then this was a less urgent matter. Students who allowed others to copy their work got little sympathy from me. Although it was a persistent and important issue that tutors enforced different standards, this was never easy to resolve. I gave the tutors detailed guidance on marking procedures, and I re-marked some of each batch of assignments to identify any tutors who needed additional help, but it was ultimately very difficult, or even nearly impossible, to impose an absolutely consistent standard.

'I shall deal with this matter', I said, and the student looked pleased, 'as soon as I have all the details. Please ask your two friends to come and see me.' He suddenly looked less happy.

I never met that student again. I shall never know whether he was merely an observer of injustice or more deeply involved.

Although my lecture classes were too large for me to know more than a miniscule proportion of the students as individuals, I identified several broad types of students, which were correlated with where they chose to sit in the lecture theatre.

The back row, which is a long way from the lectern and the blackboards, was always occupied by eighteen-year-old males who often looked bored (and perhaps were). Some of these students spent part of each lecture staring at the ceiling but, since this did not interfere with anyone else (and only I could see it), I never commented.

At the other extreme, much of the front row was always occupied by women in their fifties to seventies who were serious students and who took detailed notes. About a third of these took notes in shorthand. I remember one of these women who used shorthand to write down every word that I said, as I said it. This included every incorrect word, and its immediate correction, as I uttered them. She appeared to be recording every cough and every stutter. There was something strange about this.

Students in their twenties and thirties, and from overseas, filled a large proportion of the first ten rows. These were also serious students.

Many of the students who sat near the front recorded my lectures. This surprised me but, unlike one of my colleagues, I did not object to this. In my second year of lecturing, one of my students told me that she had been enjoying my lectures even more than she had enjoyed the lectures that I gave the previous year. I assumed that she had failed the previous year's exam, but she had not. She had borrowed tape cassettes from her sister, who had never been a university student, who had borrowed them from her cousin. I did not ask how many copies were made and whether (and at what price) they were sold.

These broad classifications of students were not rigidly defined. There was mobility between the obvious categories. A student greeted me at the end of a lecture. 'I just wanted to say that your lecture was very good today. I got more out of it than usual.'

'Thank you,' I said, genuinely pleased. 'And what was different about today's lecture?'

'Nothing,' he said with a big smile. 'It was me that was different. I have decided to work really hard. And I sat near the front.'

Of course, the lecture classes were too big but, somehow, the system worked. Most of the bored students quickly realised that making some effort would increase their chances of passing the course, and most of them achieved at least a marginal pass. Enough of these students' attitudes remained unchanged, however, to be obvious in a small proportion of my second-year students.

Students who attended my second-year lectures were set several written assignments. Details of these, including submission dates, were issued at the start of the course. The students were always told, in writing, that additional time for an assignment would not be allowed unless there was a problem that was severe, unpredictable, and unavoidable, and for which evidence was available. At the start of the course, nobody complained about this requirement.

In the week before the first assignment was due, however, I always received requests for additional time. These were always from students who sat at the back of the class.

'Until yesterday, I thought it was due at the end of the month.'

'I have written the assignment, but my dog has eaten it.'

'I'm attending my brother's birthday party tomorrow and I'll have a hangover the next morning.'

Every year, I declined almost all of these requests and, every year, almost all of the applicants accepted this with a smile. 'I knew you wouldn't allow extra time, but it was worth a try.'

A few of these students felt aggrieved.

'Other lecturers said my excuse was good enough for more time, so you should too.'

'My sixth-form teachers accepted this excuse even though they knew it was not true. Why don't you?'

Like everyone else, students have a range of attitudes. These are, perhaps, partly caused (or compounded) by the attitudes of their teachers and lecturers. And perhaps the reverse is also true. Perhaps the attitudes of teachers and lecturers are influenced by their less committed students.

11
Diminished Connections

When I became a lecturer at a New Zealand university, I had been a full-time academic for many years, but I had no experience of large-scale teaching. I had never taught in a lecture theatre with as many as 340 seats. Some of my colleagues found large classes to be stressful and several of them had done this kind of work so badly that they had been allocated to other duties. Fortunately, I found that the public-speaking skills that I needed were easier to acquire than I had feared they would be.

The large size of classes changed relationships. In my first lecturing job, I knew every student who attended my classes, and not just their names. The students in these classes knew each other. If a student missed several lectures, I would telephone. My assistance and encouragement, sometimes in difficult situations, was usually welcomed. In my new job, I knew some of the students who sat in the front row and none of the others, and a large proportion of the students were strangers to each other. At lunchtime, the communal areas of the university buildings had much in common with airport departure halls at the peak of the holiday season and with London railway stations in the rush hour.

One of my first-year students had missed a lecture because she had been unwell. At the end of the next lecture, she asked me to help her with the theory that she had missed. I suggested that she should discuss the lecture with other students, and perhaps photocopy some of their notes, before seeing me.

She looked uneasy. 'I can't do that.'

'Why not?'

'Because I don't know anyone in the class.'

This was a sad admission indeed, but her situation was not rare. Every day, I saw hundreds of students who were alone despite the crowds. Every day, I saw hundreds of students eating lunch alone, physically near other students but making no social contact. Mostly, they did not look happy.

Another student telephoned me. 'I have heard a rumour, and I want you to tell me if it's true.'

'OK. What have you heard?'

'I have heard a rumour that there are no lectures on Monday. Is it true?'

'Yes, it is true. But it's not a rumour. This information is in the course document that you were given when you enrolled.'

The student was embarrassed and apologised for interrupting my work. I said it was easy to make this kind of mistake. I did not say that his error was a symptom of declining social connections. It was interesting that, although he was a local student, he did not know that the following Monday was a public holiday. It is alarming that, although there were about nine hundred students on the first-year course in economics that year, of whom 340 attended my lectures, he had no friends, or even acquaintances, that he could ask to confirm the dates of lectures. He should also have known that this information was in the course document, of which he had a copy.

Sometimes, troubled students came to my room and wanted to tell me about their worries. They should have been telling their friends and not discussing personal matters with a lecturer who did not know them. I assume that they had no friends. I have never wanted to be a counsellor, and I have never encouraged students to confide in me but, occasionally, this non-academic role has been thrust upon me. I listened patiently, even when the problems were convoluted, and this always seemed to help. Sometimes the stories were complicated and took time to explain. I must have been doing it right because the same students often asked to see me several times before finding their way forward. Sometimes they came to tell me, months (or even a year) later, how helpful I had been. This was pleasing, of course, but I always wished that they would take their troubles to someone else.

The university provided a counselling service, for which students did not have to pay. None of the students who consulted me had considered using this service. It would be interesting to know the reasons for this. Perhaps these students were deterred by the length of the waiting list for a consultation. Perhaps they were worried whether their private thoughts would be regarded as confidential.

Some students were unsure about what was expected of them at a university. Every year, some of my first-year students asked me whether they were required to take notes during lectures. One of them said, 'You explain the subject so clearly that I can remember it without writing it down.' I always replied that note-taking was not compulsory, but that it was strongly recommended. I explained that it helped students to organise their thoughts, and that it helped them to stay engaged (and awake) during lectures. 'But nobody falls asleep in your classes,' a student told me.

Many students were suffering from inexperience of life and from being in a large complex institution where it was difficult to find friends. Such a student came to my office, looking sad and lonely. She might have been crying. She told me, hesitantly and quietly, and with a bowed head,

'I have done a very silly thing.'

My immediate thought was that she was pregnant. This was alarming to me. I am not a qualified counsellor, and I am not equipped to assist with this situation. I asked her, 'And what is the silly thing that you have done?' Luckily, I did not tell her my guess.

'I dropped my phone in the toilet and now it doesn't work'. This was a great relief to me, especially as I knew the solution to this problem. I advised her to open the telephone, to remove the battery, and to dry the parts by placing them in the sunshine for a few hours. She looked much more cheerful when she came to tell me, the following morning, that her phone was working normally again.

Some students were burdened by misguided parents. A Malaysian student came to tell me that she did not own the right kind of clothes. Her dress was long and very elegant. It was embellished with gold thread and other details. She felt acutely different from the other students. She told me that her mother had bought her a large number of new clothes, at great cost, before she left her country the previous week. I understood her discomfort.

She wanted me to advise her about the best shops where she could buy clothes that were less formal. I was not able to do this, but she was happy with my suggestion that I involve a female colleague. I spoke to one of the office staff who was about the same age as the student. She was very happy to assist. The following day, these two young women spent their lunch hour at the shops together.

The student was wearing jeans and a tee-shirt the next time I saw her. She looked totally relaxed. All of her companions, of both sexes and of several races, were dressed in the same style. And an added bonus was that the student and my young colleague became firm friends. Everyone was a winner.

I found diminishing connections to be a pervasive feature of my university work. This is also illustrated by the reactions to the collection and analysis of students' responses to their lecturers. Assembling of students' feedback on their lecturers is widespread in universities. At the university where I worked, a substantial amount of resources (including time) was devoted to this. This was intended to increase accountability of the lecturers and tutors and to increase the quality of the education that was provided. These were worthy objectives, but it is probable that they were not achieved.

Each semester, students were invited (or expected) to complete a questionnaire on each of their lecturers. They were asked whether their lecturer had helped them to learn, had communicated ideas clearly, had stimulated interest, had treated students with respect, had been enthusiastic, had held their students' attention, and had presented their lectures in a way that enabled useful notes to be taken. They were also asked to comment on the course as a whole. There were questions about the assessment methods, the course objectives, the information in the course document, and the value of the course content.

The university had many thousands of students, and the administration of these evaluation exercises was a significant activity. Each student took several courses each semester. Even part-time students probably took more than one. Each question had many possible answers, ranging from 1 ('Strongly Agree') to 5 ('Strongly Disagree') and, of course, 6 ('Not Applicable'). Detailed results were compiled, and trends were analysed. Research papers on the validity, consistency, ethics, and purposes of evaluations of university teachers were presented at conferences, published in academic journals, discussed, cited, further discussed, and almost entirely ignored.

Students asked me, every year, what was achieved by

this evaluation process. The benefit appeared to be almost zero, because the results were usually disregarded. Evaluation results might have been used, in the annual promotions process, to reward lecturers who were exceptional teachers, but the evidence that this had occurred was not obvious. They might have been used to identify lecturers who needed help to improve their teaching skills but, again, the evidence was not compelling that this had occurred. Perhaps they were used to allocate lecturers to types of teaching where they were most successful or, at least, not to roles where they were extreme failures, but there was no reason to believe that this had been done. Some lecturers could not be understood (or even heard) at the back of large lecture theatres, for example, but a costly and complex evaluation process was not needed to identify them.

Individual lecturers could opt out of the evaluation process. This was not a sound policy although, since the lecturers who could not be understood were probably grossly over-represented among the opters-out, and since very little (or no) use was made of the evaluation results, not much was lost by it.

Some of the evaluation questionnaires invited students' verbal comments on their lecturers. These comments were sent to course co-ordinators. I found these comments interesting, especially since the course that I ran had three lecture streams. It was always moving to compare comments on named individuals who taught one of the streams, such as 'He is the best in the university, knows his subject, is passionate about its importance, explains it clearly, and keeps everyone interested' and 'He's an absolute legend. Why isn't he a professor?' with comments like 'I cannot understand him. I don't even know what he is talking about', 'He should have been dismissed long ago', and 'Everyone is asleep within the first two minutes of each lecture'.

Some of these comments included explicit comparisons between lecturers. These were useful if they referred to named individuals and if they described the important attributes of a successful lecturer. When they did neither of these, however, they had little value. 'Some lecturers are better than others' was not, without more details, a helpful statement. 'My lecturer is useless' was also unhelpful. As an afterthought, the writer of this comment added 'absolutely' before the last word in this sentence which, perhaps, made it even more poignant.

Unofficial feedback occurred too, of course. I asked one of my younger students, who was a frequent Facebook user, whether he placed comments about his lecturers on the internet. 'No. What's the point? Nobody reads that stuff. Just like the questionnaires we fill in. Nobody cares what the students think.'

I was frequently reminded about the rapid evolution of universities. It was not just that they had become bigger. Individual classes had also become bigger, and lecturers had necessarily become more remote from their students. Despite this, in their increasingly intense marketing, universities usually presented themselves as being friendly and caring communities. In large institutions, however, this was difficult to achieve, and it was unlikely to have been more than a good intention.

12
Happy Families

After three years in New Zealand, which was the minimum residence requirement, Claudia and I applied for citizenship for us and for Stephen. We wanted to make a clear statement that New Zealand was now our home. This change in legal status was important to both of us, although it made no practical difference. We were, for example, already entitled to vote in local and national elections.

We had to complete forms that had many pages. There was something indefinably dated about these forms. We were asked to name the ship on which we arrived. We were required to provide the names and addresses of every school that each of us had attended since the age of five years. We were asked for details of our criminal convictions (including minor offences). There was a warning of serious consequences if any information was withheld or incomplete or fabricated. Perhaps I should have written on the form that I had been caught cheating in a spelling test in 1955.

I was aware of family issues among my students too. There is nothing constant or predictable about interactions within families and this was obvious among some of my students. Loving relationships could appear in unfamiliar ways, and it was clear that some family relationships were not loving.

One of my most diligent students, who sat near the

front at my lectures, was in his early twenties. He lived about twenty miles from the university and arrived each morning on his motorcycle. The following year, his father enrolled in the first-year courses that his son had just passed. He arrived at the university each morning on the back of his son's motorcycle. Father and son were each other's best friends.

Some of my Asian students felt under pressure from their families, especially when they had failed courses. A student told me, 'I telephoned my parents in Shanghai. They are very sad, and I do not know how to comfort them'. Another said, 'My mother will be angry. And my grandmother will be angry. I have hurt them'.

Students whose younger siblings enrolled at the university usually tried to assist them, but this was not always easy. One of my students shared a flat with her sister, who had been in my class the previous year. A few weeks into the course, the younger sister asked for my help. She wanted me to speak to her sister on her behalf. She explained that her sister made too much noise in the evenings and that this was making it difficult to study. I sympathised, but I said that I was not willing to be her advocate. I suggested that she should discuss this with her sister and, if this failed, perhaps find another place to live.

The following day, the older sister came to see me. She said that her sister was impossible to live with. She was constantly complaining. 'She says the radio is too loud, I shouldn't sing in the bathroom, and I shouldn't slam doors. You don't know my sister. She is just an old misery-guts.' And she asked me to speak to her sister on her behalf. I refused to do this. I suggested that she should try to be more considerate, but this advice was not welcomed.

I was confident that all (or almost all) of the parents of my students were interested in the progress of their offspring and, of course, I welcomed that. However, I disliked being telephoned by the parents of students who had failed exams. Sometimes these parents were almost seeking exemption from the usual procedures. These calls were particularly distasteful when it was not clear whether the student had requested, or was even aware of, the call. Such telephone calls were rare but left indelible memories.

'I am sure you know how hard-working my son is. Anyway, he got a letter this morning because he's failed his exams. Well, this is ridiculous. He has never failed any exams before. There must be a mistake. Surely you don't regard this result as reasonable? It's absurd. What were his marks in the mid-year tests? I want you to look into this and get it sorted out. I am very upset about this, and so is my son. And his father is too. Will you telephone me about this tomorrow?'

She paused for breath and, at last, I was able to get her attention. 'Any student who contacts me will receive friendly help and guidance. After payment of a small fee to the university registry, your son's examination scripts would be carefully marked again. I shall expect to hear from him soon.'

'Is that all you can say?'

'Yes.'

'Well, will you, at the very least, look at your records and tell me his test marks?'

'No. I cannot reveal confidential information about a student to a third party.'

'But I'm not a third party. I'm his mother.'

I had to summon an ambulance only once during my career. The aftermath of this also made me think about family relationships.

A student had collapsed on the steps of a lecture theatre as I was about to start speaking. I initially thought it was a joke, so I told the class that I would begin the lecture when everyone was seated, but I quickly realised that the student on the steps was unconscious.

'We need an ambulance,' I told the class. 'Has someone got a phone?' About 99% of the class immediately raised a hand. I asked a student in the front row to call an ambulance. 'Tell them they'll need a stretcher,' I said.

Every member of the class was silent when, about five minutes later, two ambulance officers arrived, lifted the unconscious student onto a stretcher, and took him to the hospital.

The disturbing part of this incident was what happened next. Nothing happened next. I had assumed that the student would quickly recover, and that he would see me to apologise for disrupting my lecture and, perhaps, to thank me for calling an ambulance. But he did not contact me. In the unlikely event of his not recovering, or not recovering sufficiently to return to the university, I had assumed that his family would contact me. But they did not.

Since the student who had been carried out of my lecture had not contacted me, I wanted to contact him. I did not know his name so, at each of my tutorials the next week, I asked the other students. None of them knew his name. I asked at the ambulance station but, on the grounds of patient confidentiality, they refused to reveal anything about him. Even his name was secret.

The absence of any subsequent contact with the student who needed an ambulance, or with any member of his family, was another stark reminder that the increasingly impersonal nature of universities was now widely regarded as normal.

There were many such incidents. A student asked me for additional time to complete an assignment. He said he had been in hospital for several days following a road accident. I did not believe him so, in his presence, and to his surprise and alarm, I telephoned the hospital. I introduced myself and I explained that I needed to know whether my student had been a hospital patient as he had claimed. The receptionist stated firmly that she would not reveal any confidential information. She did, however, use her computer to check the records and she confirmed that, the previous week, the hospital had not treated anyone with my student's surname. I told the student that he would not be allowed additional time for his assignment.

The student was amazed that I had considered his request seriously. He had assumed that I would not study the evidence before immediately agreeing to, or declining, his request. If I had not allowed extra time for the assignment, he would have been able to claim that he was an innocent and misunderstood victim of an unfeeling and inhumane bureaucracy. It was a sad reflection on today's universities, and on how they are perceived, that he was confident that my behaviour would be of such a low standard.

Sometimes students spoke to me about issues that they should have been discussing with a friend, but friends may be hard to find. Sometimes I felt that I was being treated as a parent-substitute, which made me uncomfortable, especially when the student was not much younger than me.

As exams approached, some students needed a little reassurance and guidance. A discussion of recent years' exam papers usually helped to convince them that the questions that they would have to answer would be reasonable, and that the relevant facts and theories would have been covered during the course. Some students needed only a little reassurance, while some needed much more. There was also a third type of student.

A confident man in his thirties came to see me. I

recognised him because he had often accosted me with praise at the end of a lecture. I was, he had told me several times, one of the best lecturers in the university. Now, for the first time, he had come to seek my advice.

'Basically, I am ready for the exam. I see it as an exciting challenge. But there are one or two things that I need to ask you about. I don't like to take up your time but there are just a couple of small points that I need your help with. It's difficult to explain. Although I love the subject, and I've understood your lectures, and I've learnt it all, or most of it, I don't seem to be able to integrate it efficiently into exam answers. Can you follow what I'm trying to say?'

I was not sure that I understood the problem. He was playing with his beard as he waited anxiously for my reply.

'Well,' I said, 'what are the symptoms?'

He hesitated before replying. He opened his mouth to speak and then shut it again to allow time for further thought. There was another pause before he began speaking. 'I've tried writing answers to questions from last year's exam paper. I understand the questions, or most of them, but I can't think of enough to write. After half a page of writing, I have run out of ideas. You don't get a pass mark for half a page of words, do you?'

'Not unless they are exceptionally good words,' I said with a smile. Then I realised that I had caused offence. I decided to try again. 'Let's look at a few questions from last year's exam.'

I put the exam paper on my desk. 'What about Question 8? That's a straight-forward question that you should be able to answer from the notes that you took in lectures.'

'No, I don't think I can. The lecture on this topic was months ago. It's been a long time since I read my notes.'

'How long?'

'Well, months.'

I suddenly understood, for the first time, what he had been doing all year. He had evidently been doing nothing while his classmates had been studying diligently.

'Tell me something about your study methods during the year. How many evenings per week did you spend on my subject?' He looked at the floor between my feet. He said nothing but was breathing heavily.

'Well, I ... that is, I ... you see, this is my first year at university, and I ... the fact is, I wasn't sure ... and I don't seem to have really got started in an organised way yet.'

It was obvious that he was relieved to have told someone at last. 'Look, is there any way I can master the key points in the last week?'

'Rome wasn't built in a day', I said.

13
Mutual Respect

Social changes have been substantial since I was an undergraduate student in the 1960s. This includes changes in the nature of relationships between lecturers and their students. Students have become less tolerant of lecturers whose attitudes are distasteful, and lecturers are now less frequently inclined to behave in ways that their students dislike. Lecturers are now more respectful of their students' feelings and, as a result, are respected more. Both lecturers and students are now more relaxed in the others' company.

The topic of a tutorial that I attended when I was a first-year student was mathematically complex and many of us found it difficult. The lecturer explained it carefully, covering half the blackboard with elegantly-written algebra. There was silence while we wrote it in our notes. Then the lecturer breathed an exaggerated sigh, stepped back from the blackboard, and said, 'Yes! This is the stuff to put hair on your chest!' After a brief pause, he pointed at the sole female student in the class and, with raised eyebrows and looking over his reading-glasses, he told her, 'I advise *you* not to learn this part of the syllabus'.

Although it was not funny, we knew it was a joke, so we tried to laugh. We did not know that the lecturer was going to tell the same joke the next week and the week after that. The laughter was subdued and forced the second time we heard that joke, and it was non-existent the third time. This type of humour, which was used by a significant minority of older lecturers, was a frequent irritant. But nobody complained. They would today.

Today, most students speak to their lecturers as equals. Sometimes they joke with their lecturers. This includes the oldest of their lecturers. This did not happen when I was an undergraduate.

A student approached me at the end of a lecture. This had been a demanding lecture because, following a hand injury, I had found writing on the blackboard to be difficult and painful. My writing, which had never been stylish, had become barely legible. The student was taller than me. He pointed a finger aggressively. 'You need to do something about your handwriting.' I tried to ignore the acute shooting pains in my right hand, and I started to apologise, but the student interrupted me with a laugh. He told me that he had never been able to write neatly and clearly. This banter was his way of sympathising with my ordeal.

I began another lecture by apologising for a minor error the day before. A student accosted me as I left the lecture theatre at the end of the hour. He reminded me about my error and said, 'Look, this course is hard enough even without having an incompetent lecturer'. I did not have time to begin my apology before he explained, with a big smile, that he was congratulating me for admitting my mistake.

I allowed additional time for a written assignment to a student who, less than a week before, had suffered several unexpected and distressing bereavements. She was pleased at my decision, but she was also surprised. I had refused her friend's request for additional time because it was supported with an implausible story. 'I was not expecting you to be generous', she said.

'Do not believe the rumours', I replied and, pointing to my chest, I added, 'There is warm blood in here'.

'But not much,' she said and laughed. It was probably

her first laugh since her parents and her sister had been killed by a drunk driver. That conversation and that laugh would have been inconceivable when I was a student.

Humour often lubricates social contacts but, if it is perceived to be offensive, it can have abrasive effects and can cause lasting damage. This is as true in universities as it is elsewhere.

Infrequently, and in small quantities, humour can be a useful contribution to a lecture. When I was a student, some of my lecturers never smiled. Neither did their students, even when they were awake. At the other extreme, one of my lecturers saw himself as a comedian, and persistently tried to behave as a comedian, but his students saw him as absurd and childish. He inserted deliberate errors into some of his lectures and then, the next week, made fun of the students who had not noticed these. Nobody liked him. His lectures were punctuated by buffoonery that was neither relevant nor funny, and they were regarded by the students as time-wasting and insulting. His dishonesty and trickery, despite his good intentions, were regarded with contempt. But nobody complained.

In small doses, however, occasional humour helps to maintain the students' attention and probably helps them to remember some of the lecture content. It can sometimes be used to draw attention to points that many of the students are likely to find difficult. It is also enjoyable for the lecturer. Although it is impossible to explain why, I have always found that it feels good when 340 students laugh suddenly and simultaneously, especially when the joke was not planned. A quick burst of laughter is a tonic for the students and for the lecturer but only, of course, if there have been several lectures since the last one.

Some of my former students have told me, many years after being awarded their degrees, that they could recall some of the humorous remarks in my lectures and that they had continued to use them to help in remembering difficult pieces of theory.

In my lectures, it was not only the lecturer who inserted occasional jokes. One of my tasks at the first lecture of each course was to identify the class clown. A significant minority of large classes had one. With the right response from me, he or she (but it was nearly always a *he*) could, from time to time, make a useful contribution. He might, for example, have told me when I spoke too fast. However, an unrestrained clown in the audience always had the same effect on a lecture as an unrestrained clown at the lectern. This is also a matter of respect. An irritating nuisance is an imposition, even if he thinks he is funny.

Until my public-speaking skills had improved, I sometimes found the inclusion of humour in my lectures to be difficult. In a full lecture theatre, during my first couple of months of large-scale teaching, nobody laughed when I added a humorous remark at the end of a paragraph. Without smiling, more than three hundred students wrote it in their notes. Some of them wrote it in their exam answers.

In another year, a student told me that he was repeating my course after failing the exam. He congratulated me on my lectures. He said that my lectures were even better than they had been the previous year. In a rush of enthusiasm, he went on to say that he was enjoying my wit. 'You included the same joke at the end of the fourth lecture as you did last year.'

'You can't beat the old jokes', I replied.

'You said that last year too.'

In large lecture theatres, where the back row is a long way from the blackboards, my students' note-taking was not always efficient. Students whose first language was not English sometimes had particular difficulties. I occasionally used humour to remind the students to check the accuracy of their notes. In a written assignment following my lectures on interest-rate theories, in which I had explained the significance of the supply of loanable funds, one of my students wrote, probably without trying to be clever, about the importance of the supply of 'low-level fun'. Without naming the student, I mentioned this error in my next lecture. 'There will be no low-level fun in this course,' I said.

'But I can arrange that,' said the class clown.

About three weeks after the start of the course, one of my first-year students told me 'I chose economics because the lectures did not clash with the subjects that I wanted to study. I thought economics was going to be boring. My brother did an economics course, and he said it was a boring subject. But it's not. Your lectures are good, and I'm really into economics'.

'I'm into economics too', I said, and we both laughed. Conversations like this did not happen when I was a student.

When I was the co-ordinator of a course with nine hundred students, I was the point of contact for students' complaints about their tutors. There were very few complaints but, when they happened, they were presented forcefully. Usually, a large number of students complained about the same tutor. I always took these complaints seriously. Almost all of them involved behaviour that implied some degree of lack of respect for the students.

In some years, I received complaints about tutors' lack of punctuality. Everyone understood occasional lateness because, for example, buses were not always reliable, and traffic congestion was often difficult to predict. However, the students' responses to repeated lateness were different. This was seen as inconsiderate and discourteous. Tutors were always embarrassed when I told them about the students' comments and, with one exception, the lateness ceased. The exception was a tutor that I found difficult to deal with. He was polite and apologetic when I asked him to begin his tutorials on time but, after a few weeks' improvement, his lateness recurred and got worse. Despite further requests from me, this behaviour continued, and, in some weeks, he ended his tutorials well before the due time. At the end of the year, I did not renew his contract. A large proportion of his students thanked me, but he was angry. 'Look, this is my only source of income. How would you like to be in this position?' I subsequently heard that he had been dismissed from his job in a bank because he had a serious alcohol problem. Perhaps I should have guessed this. Perhaps I should have treated my students' comments with even more urgency.

One of the difficulties that I found when preparing my lectures, when I was new to lecturing, was that I did not always know how long it would take to explain each topic, so I did not know how much content to include in each lecture-size chunk of the syllabus. This was partly because I could not accurately predict the response of the audience. It was always clear from the students' faces when they were baffled. When they stopped taking notes, I knew that I was speaking too fast or not explaining the theory in sufficient detail. It was always obvious when I needed to devote more time to a particular part of the lecture. Sometimes this meant that I had not completed my prepared lecture before the due time, when I had to vacate the lecture theatre promptly for another lecturer (and another 340 students) to enter. I liked to end each lecture with a summary of its main conclusions, but I could not include points in the summary that I had not yet covered. However, allocating the correct amount of time when preparing my lectures ceased to be a problem as my lecturing skills developed.

It was also important to have enough material to fill the allotted time. My lectures never ended early but, when other lecturers finished early, their students felt that they had been short-changed and often some of them complained about this. On the rare occasions when I reached the end of my notes before the end of the allotted lecture time, I would begin the next lecture (or preview some of its main themes) so that I did not end early. Despite the occasional unpunctual behaviour by some of my lecturers when I was a student, I do not remember any complaints of this kind.

Not everyone is happy about all the changes that have occurred, since the 1960s, in the way that universities function, but the increase in the general level of mutual respect that is seen between lecturers and their students must surely be a significant improvement.

14
Know Your Colleagues

In each of my jobs, I have had colleagues who have been friendly and supportive. Of course, this is normal among academics (and other occupational groups). Particularly when I was inexperienced, it was important to be able to discuss my work with colleagues who had improved their skills through years of practice. I have not forgotten that, until I had been lecturing for several weeks, I found each lecture to be a daunting prospect. In my first weeks of teaching, I attended some of my colleagues' lectures and observed their techniques and I learnt a lot from this. Collegiality is a reciprocal process, and I was always willing to assist younger colleagues who were new to teaching.

I have also benefitted from colleagues who were willing to comment on early drafts of each of my publications. This was an essential part of the writing process. Sometimes, I was too close to my work to be able to see its flaws. Thoughts that were clear in my head were not always included in enough detail in the text. I was always willing to provide the same kind of assistance to colleagues who needed it.

I have always found that there is something satisfying about supporting (and being supported by) colleagues. In addition to filling a need, this collegial behaviour is one of the bonuses of an academic career. However, there is some concern that recent developments mean that it is less likely to occur easily.

As universities have expanded, it is not only the relationships between lecturers and their students that have changed. Relationships among academics have also evolved rapidly. It is impossible, in a large university, to know (or even to know of) all of one's colleagues. More importantly, in large departments, it is difficult to know all of the other lecturers in the same subject area. If immediate colleagues are strangers, a source of mutual support is extinguished, and working hours might become less relaxed and less productive.

In the last generation, the unfortunate effects of larger academic departments have often been compounded by increases in the proportion of lecturers who are employed on short-term contracts and by dramatic increases in the number of part-time tutors. Social connections are more difficult when people do not have secure (or even full-time) positions. It may be particularly awkward for members of a large department at a university to get to know new recruits, and *vice versa*.

I had been working late at the university one winter evening. It was dark and it was raining heavily. I drove through the main entrance of the campus. On my left, the bus-shelter was crowded full of people trying to keep dry as they waited for their buses that had been delayed. An overflow queue had formed beside the bus-shelter. Each person was dripping with rain. Through the driving rain, I saw someone whose face and posture were familiar, so I stopped the car and offered him a ride home. He greeted me by my name, and he enthusiastically accepted my offer. He was pleased to get out of the rain. He told me where he lived, and we set off.

When I stopped the car at the next intersection, I looked at my passenger and I realised that I did not know who he was. This was disturbing. Since he knew me, my initial guess was that he was one of my students. The second semester of the academic year had just begun, and I knew none of the students who were attending my lectures, not even the ones who sat in the front row.

I was curious to know how my passenger knew me, so I asked him, 'Are you at the university?'

'Yes', he said. He seemed surprised to be asked.

I was not satisfied with this answer, so I asked him, 'Are you a student?'

He now looked very surprised. 'No. I'm not a student.'

Again, I was not satisfied with his answer, so I asked him, 'What is your role at the university?'

He squirmed in his seat. 'I'm not a student. I'm a lecturer.'

'I am too.' This made him look even more surprised.

I was still not satisfied. I wanted to know where I had met him, so I asked, 'What is your subject?'

He now looked very uneasy, perhaps even alarmed. 'Economics,' he said.

'What a coincidence. That's my subject too'.

He now looked as if he was considering leaping from the moving car to escape from a driver who was deranged and possibly dangerous.

Then I suddenly remembered that, in a crowded corridor, I had been introduced to my passenger the previous day. He had just started his first academic job after being awarded his doctorate at a university in the UK. Conversation was difficult in the lunchtime crush in that corridor. People were moving (or trying to move) in both directions, and the congestion was exacerbated by the lines of thirsty students at the coffee machines.

I was embarrassed by my error and, of course, I apologised profusely. Politely, but hesitantly, he accepted my apology. A week later, he came to see me because he wanted to apologise to me. He told me that I was only the first of several of his new colleagues whom he had met but who had not recognised him.

'I'm trying to accept this as normal,' he told me.

'At this university,' I said, 'it is normal'.

This kind of incident was unknown at the start of my career. When university departments were smaller, it was easy for colleagues to know each other and, therefore, to behave as colleagues should behave and want to behave. It is not easy to be supportive of inexperienced newcomers who are strangers. This problem has been compounded by the increased rate of staff turnover, which is due partly to the rising proportion of lecturers on short-term (including part-time) employment contracts. The benefits of universities' increased efficiency, which may be substantial when measured in financial terms (which has become normal), should be weighed against the dilution of the collegiate community.

Students also probably face greater difficulty in making social contacts and especially in finding supportive friends. This is another of the human costs of the increased efficiencies that have been achieved by increases in the scale of university classes.

In 2017, a surprising thing happened to me. Life is full of surprises, of course, but this was an exceptionally big one. I had never considered that it was a possibility. I received an e-mail from a doctor who was a student in my medical-school class when I failed all my first-year exams in 1967. I had had no contact with any of my medical classmates for fifty years, so this was a big surprise indeed. I do not know why I did not keep in contact with friends from that year. Perhaps it was part of making a fresh start after a personal disaster.

Although I had never used Facebook, Twitter, LinkedIn, or any of the other social media, one of my former classmates had found references to me on the internet and had traced my e-mail address. There were many ways in which he could have done this. He might have found details of my publications, which included several undergraduate textbooks that were listed by Amazon and by other internet retailers. Whatever the detailed explanation, it was amazing and exciting to hear from him.

He sent me the latest version of the spreadsheet showing a list of the members of the 1966-67 class, of which I was a member. This information had been revised and distributed by members of the class every few years since 1972. Initially, in those pre-internet days, it had been produced on paper, but it was now sent as an e-mail attachment. It showed the name, contact details, and a career summary of each ex-student. My name had always been on this list but, until the latest version, I had been described as 'Whereabouts unknown'. Production and distribution of this list among a group of former classmates for half a century indicated a remarkable amount of *camaraderie* that had been derived from their experiences as students.

Over the next few months, I received a flurry of e-mails from doctors who had attended lectures in anatomy, physiology, biochemistry, and other subjects in the same class as me. I was sent photographs and other memorabilia. It was heartening to know that, although my time as a medical student was brief, undistinguished, and many years ago, I had not been forgotten. Some of these former classmates recalled my acute discomfort about the prospect of a medical career and had wondered what had happened to me.

I had not correctly predicted the career paths of some of my ex-classmates. I had not guessed which individuals would become academic specialists. Perhaps it was heartening that I was not the only unlikely academic.

Courses for medical degrees are both academically and emotionally demanding. Mutual support and encouragement are important. It was indicative of this that my former classmates were still in contact with each other after so many years.

I have not lost contact with some of the people that I knew when I was an economics student, and I value this continuing friendship. I have not forgotten our mutual support. Helping them, and receiving help from them, were significant parts of my undergraduate years. I am also in contact with friends that I knew at each of my previous jobs. Again, mutual support was important. I hope that the recent evolution of universities, which has meant that I did not know, and could not know, my recently-recruited colleagues, will not weaken their collegiality so much that these types of continuing social connection diminish significantly.

15
Communication and Language

Any educational process, including university education, necessarily involves communication between the teachers and the taught. Communication occurs in both directions even when, for example during a lecture, it might appear to be in one direction only. During lectures, students' communications are mostly non-verbal. Their postures and facial expressions are likely to reveal whether they have not understood, or even cannot hear, the lecturer. More explicit communications from students include the comments that they write about their lecturers. These might be sent to the lecturers who are being commented on or, especially if they are severely critical, to someone more senior. I have always been interested to receive my students' comments on my lectures.

Since the beginning of my career, I have occasionally received comments from students who have attended my lectures. As classes have got bigger and technology has improved, the nature and frequency of these comments have changed. The content of these comments, however, has not varied much.

In my first academic job, classes were small, and I knew every student. Every year, a small but significant proportion of them sent me Christmas cards. This was encouraging. It was particularly pleasing that, each year, some of these cards included a message such as 'You're the only lecturer who doesn't send me to sleep' and 'The best lecturer!' Each year, I was always sent similar messages after the exam results were published.

These messages were a significant boost to the morale of a young lecturer. Although I knew that the students who were bored or baffled (or both), who disliked me, or who had failed exams, did not send cards, I took these greetings as an indicator of success (or, at least, of competence). I knew the requirements of a valid survey, which I had learnt thoroughly for my undergraduate exams in statistics, but I ignored them. I knew that these unsolicited greetings were not a valid indicator of students' opinions, but I received them as if I had not understood this.

Class sizes have increased dramatically and the proportion of students who send me greetings has fallen. However, I still receive unsolicited written comments.

Today's students almost always communicate by e-mail. The timing of messages is no longer constrained by the dates of Christmas, exam results, and other seasonal events. Comments arrive throughout the year, perhaps especially when assignments are about to be marked. Although I have never received an offensive comment, the students' thoughts are no longer consistently positive. The style is now often consumerist. Students, especially those who have financed their studies with large debts, see themselves as customers who are entitled to a fair deal and who expect their grievances to be heard sympathetically when they do not receive one.

Messages that were not enthusiastic about my teaching style almost always included constructive advice. 'Please slow down a bit', 'Take a breath occasionally', 'Let the slow note-takers catch up with their slow notes' and 'Think of the students who have not learnt to do shorthand' are examples. 'You speak too slowly' and 'Nobody likes those long pauses' are also examples of students' e-mails. This proves conclusively that it is not possible to please all of the people all of the time, especially in a large class.

Similar advice was sometimes given by students during lectures. I have not forgotten the student who, in almost every lecture, would, after about twenty minutes, raise a hand wearily. Then, when I had paused, he would quietly say, 'Too fast, man, too fast'. I knew this was good advice because other students always thanked me for taking it. Less frequently, but usually more assertively, a small number of students disapproved. For example, 'Don't give in to the nuisances'.

Students sometimes complained about their lecturers and, when I was a course co-ordinator, I took these complaints seriously. Unfortunately, my status in the university was not high enough to be able to take significant decisions about individual lecturers. The usual lack of any effective response from more senior people showed that students' negative comments were generally not an effective form of protest. In extreme cases of incompetence, however, the reaction of students to their lecturers was probably the catalyst, or one of the catalysts, that persuaded senior people to take difficult decisions. In these cases, lecturers were offered guidance, which they were probably unable to follow, and, occasionally, they were transferred to easier, perhaps smaller, classes.

When I was the co-ordinator of a course with nine hundred students, one of my inexperienced colleagues found a lecture theatre containing 340 students to be not merely intimidating but overwhelming. I received a large number of critical comments about him. A typical example is, 'It's not just that I don't understand what he says. I don't even know what the topic is that he is talking about. Sometimes I don't even hear him'. I deleted the students' names on these messages and then, with the agreement of the lecturer, forwarded them to the head of the department.

After a delay, during which he might have been thinking deeply about it but was probably worried about creating a dangerous precedent, he made an important decision. The lecturer was allocated to smaller classes. My incomprehensible and terrified colleague and hundreds of his students saw this as a great victory.

Following an increase in complaints about lecturers, the Students' Association at the university attempted, each year, a systematic assessment of the responses of students to their lecturers. The results of these annual surveys of students' opinions, which ran from 2000 to 2007, were published in the weekly Students' Association newsletter and were widely discussed among students and lecturers. I found the outcome of these surveys to be particularly gratifying. Four times, I was voted the Best Lecturer in the Faculty of Commerce, which, at that time, comprised about 180 lecturers. The head of my department congratulated me each time, but his comments were always subdued.

'This is not an official survey run with the authority of the university,' he reminded me one year, 'so you should not take it too seriously'.

Each time that I was a winner, I was invited to an awards ceremony and presented with an elegant certificate. Senior people in the university were invited to the ceremony but, mostly, did not attend. Perhaps some of my senior colleagues disliked the low scores that many of the students gave them.

It is a truism that effective communication cannot occur without a common language. For this reason, students whose first language was not English were required to pass a language test before being admitted to the university. Language skills were important because even small differences in language could lead to major differences in meaning. I was frequently reminded of this by my overseas students.

The majority of my students whose first language was not English were from China. They arrived at the university with a range of language skills. Some spoke and wrote excellent English. A much larger number had adequate, but not outstanding, language skills. The spoken English of a minority was difficult, or occasionally almost impossible, for me to understand. Fortunately, most of these students made rapid progress. Those whose language abilities did not improve sufficiently failed their exams because they could not write English fast enough.

Small errors of language often caused larger changes in meaning. For example, one of my Chinese students greeted me as I unlocked the door of my office one morning.

'May I see you in ten minutes?' he asked.

'Yes', I replied, so he entered my office. This surprised me until I realised that he had intended to ask, 'May I see you *for* ten minutes?'

Another Chinese student told me that the mother of one of his New Zealand flatmates had visited.

'She is a very clever woman', he said. 'Every weekend, she makes baskets. She is very generous, and she gave a big box of baskets to each of the students in the flat'.

'What are you going to do with the baskets that she has given you?' I asked.

He looked at me as if I had said something stupid. 'I have eaten the baskets,' he said. 'I have eaten all the baskets.'

This was not as alarming as it sounded. It was merely a language error. His flatmate's mother did not make baskets. She made biscuits.

Personal names are an aspect of culture that is related to language. Each year, some of my Chinese students chose a name that would be easy, for their New Zealand friends, to pronounce and to remember. These names, such as John, Margaret, Peter, Alice, did not appear on university records and were not used on written assignments and exam scripts. Some of these students asked their lecturers and tutors to use these names too.

At the end of a lecture, a student asked to see me. 'I have chosen Nicola as my name, so I hope you will call me Nicola.'

Several weeks later, the same student asked to see me again. On a sheet of paper, she had written *Nicola*, her adopted name, and she asked me, 'Is this spelling correct?' I assured her that she had written it correctly.

She looked triumphant. 'I shall tell my friend that she has chosen a wrong name.' She was about to rush off to see her friend with this information, but I asked her to tell me about her friend's name. She said that her friend had chosen Nicole and, she explained, 'Nicole is wrong. It is wrong because Nicola is right'.

Partly because I did not want to be misquoted, I told her that Nicole was the French version of Nicola and was equally correct.

'But my friend is not French. Her parents are not French. She does not speak French. She cannot use a French name.'

I explained that, in English-speaking countries, many people chose names from other cultures. Some New Zealand parents who had no French connections gave their children French names. She looked as if she did not believe me.

I wrote *Mary* on the paper. She recognised it as the name that had been chosen by one of her Chinese flatmates. Then I wrote *Maria*, and I wrote *Marie*. 'These are equally correct,' I said. 'These are the main versions of Mary that are used in Italy and in France. They are also widely used in New Zealand'.

The student looked uneasy. She was not convinced.

'In China', she said, 'all Chinese people have Chinese names.'

'But we are not in China', I said. 'It's different in Western countries.'

'Oh,' she said. I knew that she did not believe me.

Communication is of vital importance, but the message that is being sent is not always obvious to the communicator. In tutorials, I have always tried to ensure that every student had mastered each difficult point before I moved on to the next one. After discussing a tricky piece of theory, I looked at one of my weaker students and asked him if he was happy with the algebra that was on the blackboard.

'Oh yes,' he said confidently.

'Then explain it to me,' I said, and, as I had expected, he was unable to do this.

In the corridor, after the class, he asked me, 'How did you know that I had not understood that theorem?'

'I've learnt a few things about students since I became a lecturer. And I remember attending tutorials, when I was a student, that I did not fully understand.'

16
Life after University

Almost all of the students that I taught had chosen to be students. The exceptions included those who were persuaded by their parents and their teachers, against their honest judgement, to enrol in undergraduate courses. Undergraduate study was seen by almost all students as a useful method to acquire important knowledge and skills, as an enjoyable experience, as a way to find new friends, as a device to encourage employers to consider their applications for employment seriously, and, perhaps, as an excuse to move out of the parental home. However, nobody wanted to be a student indefinitely.

Early in their last year of undergraduate study, almost all of my students applied for jobs or for places to pursue further qualifications. Many did both, so that final decisions could be postponed and could be influenced by the salaries and other conditions and opportunities that had been offered by employers and by educational institutions.

Every year, but more frequently in recent years, students have asked for my advice. I have, numerous times, been invited to comment on students' draft letters to employers. The overwhelming majority of these students have needed no assistance from me other than a little encouragement. Their letters have been elegant, fluent, grammatical, and have provided appropriate information in the right amount of detail. A significant minority, however, have needed some help from me. Some have needed a lot of help.

A small proportion of the letters that I have been shown have been disturbing. Some of my students have not known how to write a letter to a prospective employer. They have not seen the need for a formal style, or they have not known how to write a letter in a formal style. If a personnel manager's name was, for example, Joseph Bloggs, it would have been better to have begun 'Dear Mr Bloggs' and not 'Hello Joe'. This was self-evident to me but, every year, it was not obvious to some of my students. Other gaffes, although less frequent, were perhaps more serious. For example, I tried to help a student who had begun each of his letters to employers with 'Have I got an offer for you?!!!', a student who had begun his letters with 'Hi there, I hope you're having a good day', and a student who ended his letters with 'Bye for now'.

The fundamental problem was that some of my students had never learnt to write a letter. Perhaps they had rarely (or never) written letters on paper. Perhaps they had rarely received such letters. E-mails and texts, which they probably sent and received frequently, are written communications that use different formats and need different writing processes from letters on paper. I have childhood memories of writing letters of thanks to an elderly aunt whom I rarely saw and did not like. She sent me gifts on my birthdays (and at other times) that I neither liked nor wanted. Nevertheless, every time this happened, I was conscripted to write to her, and I was taught how to do it. Partly because of the widespread use of telephones and the development of electronic means of communication, which have removed the need for almost all letters to be written on paper, fewer people now have this useful training. My confident guess is that letter-writing skills, which were almost universal when I was a student, have diminished severely in recent years.

In addition to their weak letter-writing skills, some of my students have had difficulty with the content of letters. The usual problem was not that they had omitted relevant information but that irrelevant facts had been included. Every year, I explained that, in addition to being a distraction, this was likely to be taken as an indicator of bad judgement. In the twenty-first century, it is probably not a wise move to describe oneself as a church member, even if it is true (and especially if it is not true). Potential employers do not need (or even want) to know candidates' marital status, height and weight, or place of birth. They are likely to be unimpressed by, for example, membership of an exclusive golf club, the number of matches played, and points scored, in a school rugby team, or an ambition to compete in the Olympic Games. Despite having sought my advice, however, some of my students were hesitant about accepting it.

Every year, I also explained to some of my students that appropriate content in a *curriculum vitae* would always have had greater impact if it had been well structured and elegantly presented. This was partly a matter of legibility and clarity. The print needed to be large enough to be easy to read but not so large that it looked ridiculous. Fancy type and coloured print would contribute nothing and were likely to be annoying. A student showed me his *curriculum vitae* that he had prepared in computer-generated copper-plate script. I advised him to choose a more conventional style of typography.

Every year, a small number of students have told me that they hoped to become lecturers. One student asked, 'What's it like being a lecturer?' This was difficult to answer in a few sentences. I was often asked about the best way to begin an academic career, and I always emphasised the importance of being awarded a PhD. Several times a year, I explained that, in economics, it was extremely unlikely that any candidate who did not hold a doctorate would be considered for a lecturing job. Of course, I would then be asked how I had managed to become a lecturer without having been awarded a doctorate. I was never sure of the answer to this. Perhaps my academic publications had been judged to be of comparable value. For almost all of my career, I have been the only lecturer in my department who did not hold a PhD. One of my students suggested that I was the last surviving member of an endangered sub-species.

Being without a PhD did not embarrass me and it led to interesting conversations with students. Whenever I was addressed using the title Dr, I always corrected this error. I did not want to be accused of claiming a distinction that had not been awarded to me. Some students had not understood the nature of this title. For example, 'You're the only lecturer that I understand. You deserve to be a Dr more than any of the others' and 'I thought that every lecturer at a university automatically got the title Dr'.

When I was a student in the 1960s, I asked other students, not my lecturers, for advice and support in connection with my applications for jobs. My letters to employers were discussed with my friends. My lecturers would probably have been surprised if I had asked for their assistance. My impression is that, sadly, some students now have no friends (or even acquaintances). Perhaps one of the consequences of large classes in large institutions is that students find it more difficult to make social contacts. The measurable benefits, especially the financial benefits, of large-scale university education are easier to assess than its social costs.

When my students applied for jobs, they needed referees, and they usually asked their lecturers. Although this had not been explicitly stated in any of my employment contracts, writing references for final-year students has effectively been an essential part of my work as a lecturer.

Most of my students have taken their studies seriously and I have been pleased to be invited to be a referee. It was not difficult to describe, in generous terms, the achievements and behaviour of these students.

A minority of those who have asked me to be a referee had been less than enthusiastic students and a small proportion of them had been academic failures. Some had been repeated failures. I have never refused to be a referee, but I have always made it clear that I would be honest. I have suggested to unsuccessful students that they should choose a different referee, and this advice has usually been accepted. When it has not been, I have tried to include comments that were encouraging (but not dishonest) beside the unfavourable information in each reference that I wrote for my weaker students. An unhappy student said, 'I can't ask any of the other lecturers because I did even fewer of their assignments than I did of yours'. This honesty, although encouraging, was not sufficient to persuade me to write a generous reference.

Occasionally, I have been asked to be a referee by students whom I had not met and did not even know of. These students had not been enrolled in any of my courses. They told me that they had heard that I was a writer of generous references, to which I always replied, 'Only when they are deserved'. I always suggested that they should address this request to one of the lecturers who had taught them. They explained to me the good reasons why they had not done this (and why they were not willing to do this).

I can recall only one student who was assertive when I suggested that he should choose another referee. 'Why won't you help me? I just need a little bit of extra help from you to get my foot on the first rung of the jobs ladder.

It's not a big ask and I'll never ask you to do it again. Other lecturers have agreed to help me, so why won't you?'

I told him that, in addition to moral issues, I needed to protect my reputation so that employers would believe me when I supported a student who was diligent, capable, and successful.

He shook his head in disbelief. 'All my other lecturers are more sympathetic.' However, I knew that at least two of my colleagues, whom he had asked to be his referees, had been equally unsympathetic.

Most of the employers to whom my students had submitted job applications asked for references to be sent in writing, but some employers have telephoned me. These telephone calls were useful because they meant that lengthy discussions of candidates' strengths and weaknesses were possible. In one of these telephone calls, I was told that I should be uninhibited because the conversation would be strictly off the record. When I asked, 'Is it not being recorded?' the reply was incoherent.

A small proportion of employers have not asked for written references but have sent me forms that they have asked me to complete. Some requests for written references have been accompanied by forms to be completed. These forms have not been all the same. Some were a single sheet of paper that could be completed quickly. Others had many pages and included questions to which I did not, and could not, know the answers.

Early in my career, I tried to answer every question, however silly, on the forms that had been sent by my students' prospective employers. Later, however, my policy was not to answer questions that were absurd. This approach did not appear to reduce my students' chance of success in the employment market.

I knew it would probably damage my students' interests, so I always avoided humour when completing forms from employers. For example, when I was asked, on the Personal Attributes section of one of these forms, 'Is he/she a good mixer?' I did not reply, 'Yes. He stirs things up well'.

A small proportion of employers' requests for references referred to students who had not sought my permission. This was an irritant, as I explained to each of these students. It is interesting that 100% of the students who quoted my name as a referee without first asking me were unmotivated and academically weak. Some of them had failed exams. I encouraged every one of them to choose another referee, but I did not refuse to write references.

Most employers probably attach little value to the content of references because they cannot assess them. Who are the referees' referees?

17
Conflicts of Interest

In the last generation, universities have made strenuous efforts to be welcoming to all social groups. It has been seen as important to increase (and celebrate) the enrolment of students who were members of under-represented social groups. These disadvantaged groups have been defined by gender, race, age, parental income, disability, sexuality, or something else. These under-represented groups included the parents of young children.

Despite good intentions, children and universities have been an uneasy combination. People of all political opinions have agreed that family responsibilities are important and should be respected, but the practical applications of this have not always been straightforward.

A student asked my permission to bring her four-year-old son to a tutorial. She explained that her son's grandmother, who usually looked after him when she was attending classes, had been hurt in a road accident and was now in hospital. She was very keen not to miss any of my tutorials. She promised to take her child outside the room immediately if he distracted the class, so I reluctantly agreed.

In the tutorial room, the students sat at tables that were arranged in a square. The child sat on the floor in the middle of the square. His mother had brought some of his favourite toys, including several cars, a police car, and a fire engine. To my great relief, the child knew how to behave. He had obviously been in this kind of situation many times. He knew that he was not allowed to interrupt the adult conversation. He was quickly absorbed into the world of his toys.

I began the tutorial. Although the room was quiet, it was clear that, unlike each of my earlier tutorials with this class, nobody was listening to me. The students were watching, and listening to, the child. In a whisper, he was telling a story. 'Look, there's been a smash ... Is anyone hurt? ... Look, another car has hit the smash ... Has somebody called the police? ... Oh good, here comes the police car ...' In a whisper, he imitated the sound of a police-car siren. Everyone wanted to know the outcome of the story. Did the police arrest the dangerous driver? Why was he speeding? Did the ambulance get the injured to the hospital in time? This week's assignment in economic theory could not compete for the students' attention.

This was a difficult situation. Had the child been rowdy, or attention-seeking, I would have asked his mother to remove him, but he was doing nothing wrong. He was doing everything that he had been taught to do, and I approved of his having been taught to behave in this way. I was unable to say anything critical to the child's mother or to him. Although the presence of a four-year-old child made this tutorial interesting and unusual, and a good thing to talk about over lunch, it was, as an educational exercise in economic theory, a complete waste of my time and of the students' time.

Another student brought her three-day-old baby to a tutorial. She promised to take him outside if he made a sound. Again, I reluctantly agreed, and he was placed, in his carry-cot, in the middle of the square of tables. He was asleep, which was reassuring. It was impossible that he would be a nuisance.

I felt very sympathetic to the mother of this baby

because she was an exceptionally diligent student. She had attended 100% of my lectures. She always sat in the middle seat of the front row, looking up into my nostrils. She always listened carefully to every part of each lecture and took lots of detailed notes. Over many weeks, I had observed her getting bigger as her pregnancy progressed. At the start of my lecture the previous Friday, she told me that her doctor had advised her to rest at home with her feet up, but that she had not wanted to miss any of my lectures. She was so large that she was walking very slowly, obviously worried about falling. I thought that her doctor had given very good advice but, since I am not a doctor, I made no comment. During that lecture, she suddenly put down her pen, and started breathing heavily, with her head back and her mouth open, and closed her eyes tightly as if in pain. I was about to telephone for an ambulance. Then, equally suddenly, she recovered her composure, sat up straight, opened her eyes, picked up her pen, and started writing again, so I continued the lecture. Her baby was born that afternoon at the hospital, which was a much better place for this to happen.

And, three days later, she brought her son to my tutorial. Nobody could accuse this baby of being disruptive. He did nothing. He was asleep. Despite this, the tutorial was a waste. Nobody listened to me, or even looked at me, as I explained the first line of algebra on the whiteboard.

After a few minutes, most of the students had realised that the baby was doing nothing, and was going to do nothing, and so they had started listening to me. Then he sneezed. This was not a loud sneeze, or a prolonged sneeze, or a repeated sneeze. This was the kind of sneeze that would be expected from a three-day-old who is asleep. But it was enough to destroy my tutorial. The students who had been following my algebra were determined not to miss the next sneeze.

As she left the room at the end of the hour, the student said that her son's name should be in *Guinness World Records* as the youngest person to have attended a university class. At my tutorials, there were, fortunately, no other candidates for this title.

Many of my colleagues did not allow their students' children to attend their classes. Although I have found it difficult to do this, there were powerful arguments for excluding children. Some of my colleagues have been concerned about the safety of students' children. Others felt that it was unreasonable for students to impose their parental responsibilities on lecturers, on tutors, and on other students. My opinion is that, as a matter of university policy, lecturers and tutors should be strongly discouraged from allowing children to attend their classes. Perhaps they should not be permitted to allow children to attend lectures and tutorials. There might be safety issues, particularly in laboratories, but this is not merely an issue of safety. Lectures and tutorials require the whole of the attention of the teacher and of every student who is present. They are not social events to which family members can be invited and, if necessary, students should be reminded of this. Undergraduate education is paid work for the lecturers and tutors, and it should also be regarded as work, and not a hobby or a social activity, by the students. There are many similar situations. For example, I do not want my dentist's child to be present while my teeth are being drilled. When I travel by bus, I do not want a child to share the driver's seat.

Universities' publicity material frequently includes descriptions, in generous terms, of the assistance, including childcare, that is available for parents. However, to be genuinely welcoming to students who are parents, universities need to ensure that the facilities that they run are big enough, with adequate staffing and in convenient locations, and at low (or zero) cost. Overcrowded facilities, with long waiting lists, are not sufficient.

Despite all of these arguments, I have found it difficult to refuse a request to bring a child to one of my classes. When I said to a student that bringing her three-year-old child to a lecture (and expecting her to remain still and silent for an hour) was an act of child cruelty, she thought that I was trying to be funny. Her daughter remained silent for about four minutes from the start of my lecture and, fortunately without an explicit request from me, she took her outside. The following day, she came to my office to apologise for not taking my advice.

There have been other kinds of conflicts of interest in my university work. At the start of each academic year, a significant minority of my first-year students have been surprised to discover that, in addition to attending lectures, they were expected to attend tutorials. Such students often have not understood the concept of a tutorial, at which a small group of students would meet regularly with a tutor. Some students have been surprised that participation in tutorial discussions was not only permitted, it was required. In some of these students, this prospect has caused a feeling of panic.

The nature of tutorials varied between academic subjects, but the usual practice was that students were set an assignment in advance and were expected to be able to discuss this at a tutorial. In the first-year courses that I taught, each tutorial assignment needed about an hour's work before the class, and some of them involved calculations. Students were told that they were expected to attempt the assignment, in writing, before attending each tutorial.

Every year, at the first lecture, I reminded students about the nature of a tutorial. 'If you have not done the assignment, you will not get any value from the tutorial. You will not even understand the discussion. Do not expect to be entertained by the other students. You will not be able to contribute if you have not done the work.'

Every year, at my first tutorial, despite my assertiveness at the first lecture, a substantial proportion of the students had not attempted the assignment. Sometimes more than a third of the students had not even looked at it. Most of these looked sheepish when I reminded them of their obligations, but some fought back. 'My sixth-form teachers said that sort of thing but never meant it.' 'My friend said you don't really need to do the assignments.' 'I did my assignment but left it on the bus.' 'It's on my computer which was stolen yesterday.'

The students who had not prepared for their first tutorials were always, as I had predicted, unable to participate. Some of them tried to write down every word that was said, by me and by the students who were actively involved, even if they had not understood these words. They were usually unable to write fast enough. It was the same every year.

At the second tutorial each year, the proportion of prepared students always increased. Sadly, however, attendance always declined markedly and never recovered. The absent students were, of course, the non-participants. These were probably the students who had the greatest need for the educational benefits that were derived from tutorials. The only solution to this paradox is to specify a course requirement of a minimum number of tutorial attendances. Unwilling conscripts, however, are probably thinking about other things. They say nothing and learn almost nothing. They can be compelled to bring their bodies to tutorials but not their minds.

In the first week of each course, I was always asked whether attendance at tutorials was compulsory. My reply was always the same. In the courses that I taught, it was expected but not required. I added that tutorial attendance was likely to increase the chance of passing the exam. I was probably not believed. I said that most students enjoyed their tutorials. I was almost certainly not believed. I said that attendance at lectures was also not compulsory, to which the usual reply was 'Why would anyone want to miss your lectures?' I could never think of a good response to that.

Sometimes, I told these students that attending the exam was not compulsory. This always produced gasps of amazement. I explained that the consequence of not attending the exam was a 100% chance of a failure grade. The consequence of not attending tutorials was also a failure grade, but with a lower percentage chance. I was never believed. I hoped that these conversations had been remembered when the course results were published.

18
Curing Brain Murk

Universities are seasonal institutions. The teaching year is shorter than the calendar year and research activity is often concentrated in the non-teaching times. Some of my colleagues detested teaching, and disliked having anything to do with students, and they celebrated the end of each semester. They could then make progress on their research without interruptions. My attitude was different. As each new semester approached, I looked forward to seeing the students again. There was also an annual cycle in some of the administrative procedures of the university, including the enrolment and graduation of students. The seasonal role that lecturers usually did not enjoy, and often dreaded, was the marking of exams. The loathing of exam marking was particularly acute when the exam had been sat by students on a large first-year course.

For many years, I was one of the markers of the exam at the end of the first-year course in economics. Each year, there were about nine hundred candidates, and each marker was responsible for one question. Every exam had a choice of questions, and no question was attempted by all nine hundred students. Marking was allocated according to the pressure of each marker's other commitments. A lecturer who was also marking the exams for more advanced courses might be allocated a question that had been attempted by fewer than fifty students. For several years, when I was a newcomer to the university, I was required, each year, to mark a question that had been attempted by more than eight hundred students.

Reading the first ten answers in a batch of exam scripts was always interesting. It was encouraging when students had understood complex theory and could explain it clearly, even under exam conditions. It was interesting, in a different way, when students tried to convince the markers that they had understood and remembered more than they had. These attempts at deception were never successful. The next twenty answers in the pile of exam scripts were slightly boring. The same successes, the same failures, and the same attempted deceptions, occurred again and again and again. The rest of the allocated answers, of which there were probably at least five hundred and possibly more than eight hundred, were just a tedious and meaningless slog that went on and on and on and on. The dreary and repetitive nature of the content of the answers that students had written in exams was often compounded by their difficult handwriting. I sympathised with the students, especially since I had always had problems making my handwriting neat and legible. I also remembered that I had found my undergraduate exams to be very stressful, and I knew that my exam answers had not shown the full extent of my knowledge and understanding of the subject. Nevertheless, hour after hour after hour of deciphering inelegant (or almost illegible) handwriting made a wearying chore even more wearying.

During the exam-marking season, every year, one of my colleagues always told me that he was suffering from Brain Murk. The defining feature of Brain Murk, which was evidently a psychological condition, was the unshakeable conviction that one's brain was turning murky and ceasing to function properly. The only effective therapy, which would have caused the symptoms to disappear immediately, was to stop marking exam answers.

However, contractual obligations to the university, and moral obligations to the students, meant that this therapy was not possible. But, every year, continuing the marking caused the symptoms to worsen, probably at an accelerating rate.

In their exam answers, a small proportion of students mentioned their lecturers. These comments were interesting, truthful, amusing, or none of these. Perhaps by relieving boredom, these comments reduced the severity of the marker's Brain Murk. They were rarely unkind. Students knew that it would probably be unwise to insult the marker. Examples are 'As Jerry Mushin, the famous author, says …' and 'I learned this topic from the textbook by Jerry Mushin. I couldn't understand the other books we were told to read.' Reading these comments always improved, but did not cure, my Brain Murk.

The best students did not uncritically learn the content of the lectures that they had attended. For the highest marks, students needed to show that they had thought about the course content, that they could compare alternative views, and that they could describe weaknesses in the theories that were explained in lectures and in textbooks.

In one of my lectures, when I was not experienced in large-scale teaching, I muddled a piece of theory, but did not notice the error in my notes for several weeks. Partly because it was only a small error, I did not tell the students about my mistake. Of course, I immediately regretted this (and, when I was more experienced, I always admitted my errors as soon as I became aware of them). At the end of the course, about eighty students showed that they had learnt the muddled theory that I had presented by including it in their exam answers. Fortunately, I was the marker of that question. As I was new in the job, a senior colleague had been instructed to check my marking. He assured me that he had done this and that I had set the correct standard in my marking. I was not convinced that he had examined all of the evidence before reaching this conclusion.

Exams are, of course, a contentious issue. The ethics and practicalities of exams have been extensively discussed for many years or even, probably, many decades. Everyone agrees that exams are stressful for the students. For some students they are extremely stressful. I was such a student, and I have clear memories of this. Everyone agrees that exam marks are not always an accurate measure of the students' knowledge and understanding of their subject. This is partly because of the stressful nature of exams. Finding a workable substitute for written exams, however, is not a simple matter.

When I was an undergraduate student, the assessment for my degree was entirely by means of exams. Each exam lasted three hours. We were set regular written assignments, including long essays that took weeks to complete, and most students attempted most of them (and I suspect that most of the remaining students attempted all of them). However, the function of this written work was purely educational. It was not part of the assessment. A lot has changed since the 1960s, and it is now usual for course-work marks to be included in assessment.

Supporters of the use of course-work marks for assessment have claimed strongly that it reduced students' exam-stress. The counter-argument to this has also been expressed strongly. Many of my colleagues have been concerned that, due to the inclusion of every assignment mark in their final grades, students now experience stress throughout each course and not just before and during exams, so attempts to reduce stress have compounded it.

Another argument was that course-work assessment was likely to be more accurate than exams as a measure of academic achievement. This was also controversial. One of the major issues was that course-work was impossible to police. We could not be certain who had written each assignment. Some students received a little help, or even a lot of help, from friends and family. Some of them admitted this after their degrees had been awarded. It was possible that some students had paid to have assignments written for them, but nobody ever admitted this so there was never any evidence.

Another issue was that, when assignments were marked by tutors, of whom there were a large number, and not by lecturers, it was impossible to ensure that they were all marking to the same standard. It was also possible that the same piece of written work had been submitted to numerous tutors (and the marks credited to individual students). However, if assignments were marked by lecturers, and not by tutors, this was certain to make the problem of Brain Murk even more serious. All of my colleagues were worried about any policy that would increase the incidence and the severity of Brain Murk.

Assessment could also be based on multiple-choice test scores. These tests could be marked by computer and so there would be no risk of Brain Murk. Preparing these tests would take longer than preparing conventional exams but, since the burden of marking (and of Brain Murk) had disappeared, there would be a substantial net gain for lecturers. However, although multiple-choice tests have been used increasingly in universities, especially for large first-year courses, there has been considerable doubt about whether this form of assessment can be a valid measure of students' success in their university education. It has always been difficult to devise multiple-choice questions that adequately tested students' ability to think about the theory that they have learnt.

Even for those lecturers who have experienced the most severe symptoms of Brain Murk, exam marking was not always unrelieved drudgery. One of my students wrote the first paragraph of the answer to an exam question, but then crossed this out, turned to a new page, and began the answer to a different question. Before abandoning his first answer, however, he wrote at the bottom, 'I attended Jerry Mushin's lectures, and I don't think he finds this topic any easier than I do'. I was pleased that the student had remembered me and that he had not been just an automated and mindless note-taker. This was the best cure for Brain Murk.

19
Textbook Issues

My first-year students quickly discovered that they needed textbooks. Remembering what lecturers had said, even if it had been understood, and even if their memories had been accurate, was never sufficient to pass exams. The lecturer's roles included encouraging students to read textbooks and helping them to learn from textbooks. The textbooks' roles included helping students to understand, and learn from, their lecturers. Although this symbiotic relationship has not changed, the nature of textbooks has changed considerably since I was a student.

Many of today's textbooks, especially for first-year students, are designed to be exciting. Although, when I was a student, publishers did not want their books to be boring, they were not designed to be thrilling and sensational in the way that they often are now. An American publisher describes its textbooks as 'motivating'. Recent textbooks, especially those intended for first-year students, are usually illustrated with numerous pretty pictures, in bright colours, which are often of limited relevance to the content. There are also likely to be cartoons, anecdotes, references to American films and television series, and other gimmicks. I assume that these are intended to assist the less able, revitalise the bored, energise the lazy, and arouse the somnolent. A large number of my students have commented on this type of textbook. They have found this style to be irritating and insulting. Some of these comments have been very assertive.

'If I want cartoons, I'll buy a newspaper.'

'He never uses four words when eighteen will do.'

'I am not a child, and I dislike being treated as if I am.'

'The cartoons are not relevant, helpful, or even funny.'

Another feature of recent textbooks for first-year students of economics, which I do not remember occurring when I was a student, is that some of their authors have confused theory and opinion. Sometimes, their authors' political views are presented as generally accepted theory. Many of my students have resented this.

'He assumes that his readers are ignorant and uneducated.'

'He should not tell students what to think.'

'He does not understand the difference between theory and ideology.'

'A textbook should include different approaches.'

Although this did not generally occur when I was a student, almost all publishers now produce supplementary material to accompany each textbook. Sometimes this is limited to brief guidance and suggestions, related to each chapter, for lecturers. I would have been grateful for this kind of assistance when I was an inexperienced lecturer. My younger colleagues have usually been pleased to receive this type of resource. However, some publishers do much more than this. For example, they provide extensive assessment questions, including hundreds of pages of multiple-choice questions. My colleagues' responses to this have been varied. Some lecturers have welcomed assistance with tedious tasks that they could not avoid. Others have complained that their jobs have been de-skilled. Even those who have used the publishers' test questions have been aware that these have constrained the content of lectures and have restricted their academic freedom (which is often seen as almost sacrosanct).

A significant number of publishers issue (to lecturers only) a set of detailed notes for each lecture. All my colleagues have consistently disliked this, but some have used these notes anyway. The lecturers who have done this have tended to be those who have regarded their teaching responsibilities, and their students, as time-consuming distractions from their research work. These lecturers have welcomed all opportunities to reduce the time that they devote to the preparation of lectures.

Since the late 1990s, publishers' notes for lecturers have usually been accompanied by PowerPoint slides. These are elegantly produced and in many colours. They have included complex graphs that describe theoretical models. Some of my colleagues have used these in lectures; the saving in preparation time can be substantial. But I have never used publishers' PowerPoint graphs in my lectures. Instead of presenting the students with complete diagrams, which are probably overwhelming in their detail, I have used large blackboards to construct complicated graphs, step by step, as each lecture progresses. I have explained and discussed each part of each diagram, as I have drawn it. This approach has enabled students to understand the theory and has helped them to remember it.

The students' responses to my teaching have mostly been enthusiastic. On evaluation forms, students have written comments that have encouraged me not to use publishers' prepared material to illustrate my lectures. 'Lecturers who use PowerPoints send me to sleep. Jerry Mushin's style is much more interesting.' 'There is never enough time to copy the PowerPoint slides in lectures into my notes. In some lectures, they are on the screen for only a few minutes. They are far too complicated to understand quickly, and I give up trying. The animations do not help. I prefer Jerry Mushin's style. He takes a whole lecture to draw two (or three) diagrams, talking about them as he does it. Hurrah!'

Market pressures have been the driving force behind the rapid evolution of textbooks. Publishers have produced whatever books have sold best. Competition has been fierce, especially at the first-year undergraduate level, where classes are generally very large. Textbooks have often been chosen not by lecturers but by more senior people who have had little direct contact with first-year students, and this might have compounded the problem.

Revised editions of textbooks have been published frequently, sometimes annually. Although these new editions have included improvements and updating, they have been mostly rearrangements of the existing content. Changing the order of chapters, the size of pages, and the number and location of illustrations are attempts to destroy the second-hand market for textbooks. When I was a student, buying used textbooks at the start of the year and selling them at the start of the next year benefited all parties (except the publishers). This is more difficult now because lecturers are likely to refer to the page numbers and other details of the latest edition (or perhaps the latest two editions) only. Most students now want to buy only the latest version of each textbook.

The conclusion of Darwinian theory is that species evolve because the fittest survive. This applies to textbooks but only in terms of publishers' profits. Quality is often a casualty. American military commentators would call it collateral damage.

The functions of universities include encouraging and enabling students to consider a wide range of opinions and approaches and to form their own. Good textbooks help students to do this and so do good lectures. The best lectures and the best textbooks complement each other but they are not, and should not be, identical. Unfortunately, where the differences in content are significant, some first-year students have difficulty balancing confidence in their textbooks with confidence in their lecturers. This is partly because some textbooks do not devote sufficient attention to theories that their authors dislike (and perhaps that the students' lecturers have included and discussed). My guess is that the proportion of lecturers whose teaching style is similar to these books is probably small but not insignificant. More frequently, however, the problem is due to (probably a small minority of) students becoming excessively loyal to their usual textbooks, with which they are familiar. This makes them less willing to consider any views that the books dismiss briefly or do not include. This might be encouraged by intensive advertising by textbook publishers.

Some students develop a more general loyalty to textbooks. They assume that anything that is published in a book must be valid and *vice versa*. The content of lectures might not be totally respected by such students if it is inconsistent with, or clearly different from, their textbooks. This became apparent when, each year, I presented a first-year lecture on a particularly complex piece of theory. Many of the students found the algebra difficult to follow. I understood how they felt because this topic had baffled me when I was a student. At the next lecture, therefore, each year, I explained the same theory again, but I replaced the algebra with a numerical example. This held the attention of the students and, each year, at the end of the lecture, a large number of them thanked me. However, there were always a few students who were uncomfortable that my example was not in their textbook.

'Thank you for using the numerical exercise. It was really clear and helpful. I was able to follow it through to the end. But it's not in the textbook. I want to read more on this. Which book did you get it from?'

'It is not from a book. I wrote it myself.'

The student looked alarmed. 'Are you allowed to do that?'

'Yes, I am allowed to do that. I'm a lecturer at a university. That is my job. It's what I get paid to do.'

I smiled, so the student smiled too. But he looked very uneasy.

When lecturers and textbooks tell different stories, some students show excessive loyalty to their lecturer. A group of my students from China were waiting patiently outside my office when I arrived one morning. They said that they had enjoyed my lecture the previous day but were worried because the content was not exactly the same as the textbook.

'You described a different way to the textbook. Which is correct? Which should we learn? Your way or the textbook?'

'Learn them both. Or learn whichever you prefer. Both are correct. The conclusions are the same. You can decide which is easier to understand.'

'But please tell us which is better. You know which is better. You are our teacher.'

Attitudes to lectures and textbooks were always complicated by exams. Every year, a few students asked me whether the exam questions would be based on the textbook or on the lectures. And, every year, my reply was the same.

'The exam is designed to test students' knowledge of the syllabus, not their knowledge of the textbook or of the lectures. The exam questions will be related to the textbook, or to my lectures, or to both, or to neither. You will get a pass-mark if you have sufficient detailed knowledge of the subject and can explain it clearly under exam conditions.'

This reply always caused great concern and

occasionally a hint of panic. I did not know how to help students to become more judicious in their attitudes to their textbooks and to their lecturers.

20
Academic Publications

Every lecturer's employment contract refers to research activity and the publication of its results. Universities are not just teaching institutions.

Although my thesis was not a success, I learnt a considerable amount about research methods when I was a Research Assistant. I have also learnt from academic colleagues in my subsequent jobs. I have applied this knowledge to my research work since becoming a lecturer.

I have had to abandon some of my research projects before they were completed. It is always disappointing to cease work on an interesting topic, especially if the work is well advanced but, if sufficient data are not available, or if someone else has published the same ideas and conclusions, it may be the only option. Fortunately, I have been able to complete most of the projects that I have begun.

Academic publications are the usual indicator of successful research activity and universities keep records of the published output of each of their staff. This information is used in promotion decisions and in the appointment of new staff. However, it is not easy to assess this information in a consistent way. Some publications are better, longer, more interesting, more theoretical, more detailed, more rigorous, or more mathematical, than others. The merit of the research output of a particular lecturer cannot be measured merely by counting the number of publications.

Although the publication of research results is a contractual obligation, there is usually little (or no) accountability for lecturers who rarely (or never) do this, or whose publications are short or trivial. There is no measure of research success which is generally agreed to be valid. This is a conundrum that universities have yet to solve.

It is obvious that some academic journals have higher status than others. However, using this concept to apply a weighting to each published article is not easy. There is widespread disagreement about the appropriate placing of each journal in this prestige ranking.

In almost every article, academic authors include references to related publications in the same area. Detailed records are kept of these citations, and these can be consulted on several internet sites. However, the number of citations is also not always a sound measure of the level of academic achievement of an author. One of the reasons for this is that it is impossible to monitor. It is possible that some authors ask their friends to cite their publications and, of course, are willing to return this favour, thus increasing the citation counts of all of them.

Although my main interest has been in teaching, I continued with my independent research when I became a lecturer. Many of my articles have been on exchange-rate systems and on the interaction of exchange-rate policy and domestic macroeconomic policy.

In 1993, a first-year student said, 'Your lectures are better than the textbook that we've been told to buy. You could convert your notes into a textbook. Why don't you write a textbook?' That conversation reminded me that, about fifteen years earlier, I had begun writing a textbook. The first chapter was still in my filing cabinet. I decided to follow my student's advice and try again.

After substantially more effort than I predicted it would need, my first textbook was published in 1994. It differed from other textbooks in its style (which included no gimmicks and only minimal algebra) and in its content (which referred to New Zealand data and institutions). It was enormously satisfying to see it in bookshops. The head of my department congratulated me but only quietly and with the caveat that 'it's just another textbook for first-year students'.

I was no longer the co-ordinator of the first-year course in economics, which had about nine hundred students, and I did not succeed in persuading my successor to adopt my textbook. However, despite this, I exercised my academic freedom and recommended it to the 340 students who attended my lectures. A month later, I was pleased to hear from the manager of the university bookshop that about five hundred copies of my book had been sold there. This was very pleasing especially since it is unlikely that my book was bought by all of the students that were in my lecture stream.

Improved and extended editions of my book were published in 1996 and in 1999, and similar quantities were sold. Then there was a major revision of the first-year syllabus in economics that I was required to teach. This destroyed the market for my book. I was involved in the lengthy discussions that preceded this change and, with many of my colleagues, I opposed it strongly. Ultimately, however, I was on the losing side. Partly because I was working on other projects, and partly because I disliked the innovations, I decided not to write a textbook that matched the new syllabus.

One of the interesting features of having work published is that one thing leads to another. This has applied both to my articles in academic journals and to my books. It is most encouraging that several adaptations of my textbook have been published.

In 2001, a revised and shortened version of my book, intended for use in secondary schools, was published in the UK. I prepared this with a long-standing friend (who had been one of my colleagues in the 1970s).

In 2002, a revised version of my textbook was published for the United States market (and to be used in other countries). This was an elegant hardback book. I replaced the New Zealand data with American data and improved some of the content. In an enthusiastic e-mail, the publisher's marketing manager wrote, 'I know this one is going to be a million-seller. I can feel it'. Unfortunately, he was wrong. Only a small number of copies were sold, and it was not reprinted.

A Chinese translation of the United States version of my textbook was published in Beijing in 2004. Although, or perhaps because, I was unable to read it, this was most gratifying. One of my students from China imported a large number of copies of this book and sold them to his compatriots. Many of his customers asked me to sign their copies. One of them said, 'It is an honour to meet a famous economist like you'. I said that I was not a famous economist, but he did not believe me.

A revised and updated version of my textbook was published in India in 2009. This was also a hardback book. I substituted Indian data for the New Zealand data and improved the presentation of some of the theory.

An Australian edition of my textbook was published in 2015. I included additional improvements and Australian data.

A lecturer was appointed by my publisher to prepare the revisions for the Nigerian edition of my textbook that was published in 2019. My relationship with the co-author of this project was an interesting application of digital technology. We communicated entirely by e-mail. On numerous occasions, she asked me to comment on a few pages (or a few paragraphs) that she had written, and I always sent my response quickly. My comments were always immediately acknowledged. Without e-mail, in view of the frequent delays in the international postal system, this project would have been arduous or even unworkable. My co-author's e-mails to me also included interesting insights into the life and work of a lecturer at a Nigerian university. This was an added bonus.

My academic publications include two articles in the *Encyclopedia of Economic and Business History*. This is an internet resource which was (and is) still in its infancy. It is intended for educated but non-specialist readers. I wrote, in 2006, about the development of the euro and, in 2012, about the Sterling Area. I have revised and updated my articles several times. Each year, I have received numerous e-mails from readers of these articles, which is encouraging. Although most of these e-mails have been from undergraduate students in the United States who have been requested to read one of my articles before preparing a written assignment, about 30% of them come from other countries. Soon after my second article was published in the *Encyclopedia of Economic and Business History*, I was invited to become a Consulting Editor. This was (and is) an interesting role. I am asked to comment on articles that have been submitted to the *Encyclopedia* and, where this is necessary, to edit them.

In 1999, I was invited to contribute a chapter to a textbook to be published by the New Zealand Journalists Training Organisation. This textbook dealt with the economic issues that journalists were likely to encounter in their work. My chapter was about some of the significant recent controversies in macroeconomic policy.

In 2010, the head of my department encouraged each of his colleagues to register with the Social Science

Research Network, which runs an internet site that indexes the abstracts of articles in academic journals. He explained that this was needed as an essential part of the department's marketing effort. I assumed that there would be no benefit to me, but I was mistaken. The effect has been that I have received e-mails from academic researchers in many countries whose publications (and work in progress) are in related areas to mine. Some of these enquiries have led to my publications being cited in articles in academic journals.

Listings of my articles on other internet sites have also encouraged academic authors to write to me and to cite my work.

There is nothing new about an academic author being contacted by readers, but the development of e-mail and of indexing sites on the internet have made these contacts easier and much more frequent.

I have no delusions about the importance of my academic publications. I shall not be remembered as a significant economist. Nevertheless, I have derived enormous satisfaction from seeing my work in print. Citations and encouraging comments from other authors have contributed to this. Every one of my publications has made a (small) contribution to the subject that had not already been written about.

Some of my students have been impressed by the number of my books that were in the university library. I have explained many times that my publications were not of exceptional merit, and that a library holding was not a great honour. A typical response was, 'Don't be so modest. They must be good books, or they would not be in the library.'

21
Explosive Growth of Marketing

Information published by, and about, universities has changed dramatically since I was a student in the 1960s. At that time, the booklets that were issued by universities were brief, had only a few pages, and included no photographs. The intention was to assist potential students to make informed choices by providing an accurate summary of the content and entry requirements of each of the courses that were available. There were sufficient details but no gimmicks.

The publicity output of today's universities is entirely different. Booklets are now large and lavishly illustrated with pictures in bright colours on every page. They are designed to attract customers rather than to inform enquirers. Information is still included, but it may be difficult to find among the other content. Prospective students can read about recreational facilities, accommodation, the international reputations of some members of the academic staff, the successful careers of recent graduates, the prominent and successful people who have studied at the university, the history of the university, and even the host city.

It is not just the printed publicity material that has changed. Universities now place frequent advertisements in newspapers and magazines, on buses and bus shelters, on hoardings, and on television. This advertising continues throughout each year. Even campuses are not exempt. The public parts of university buildings now include advertising slogans and animated screens. There is no escape from the constant repetition of slogans. Marketing efforts never sleep.

Each university also devotes a large amount of attention to its corporate identity. Logos and branding are carefully designed, and frequently changed, for maximum impact. Headed paper and signs on buildings are redesigned to be consistent with the latest branding improvement. Names of institutions and of their parts are changed if there is perceived to be a marketing advantage.

Universities generally run at least one Open Day each year. The arrangements vary but it is usual that each department provides lectures and demonstrations that are related to its courses. Members of the academic staff are available to answer questions.

I have presented several Open Day lectures on behalf of my department. The audiences had little in common with my usual undergraduate lecture classes. There were always large groups of seventeen-year-olds, who were accompanied and shepherded by their teachers. Many of these teenagers behaved as if they were unwilling conscripts, and perhaps they were. Some of these groups had boarded their buses before midnight and, having enjoyed the journey, were now ready for sleep. The teachers looked tired too. I never enjoyed lecturing at Open Days. Speaking to people who are sleepy, not interested, and probably bored was not appealing. There were always persistent whisperers and gigglers and a large number of late-comers. Of course, not everyone (or even a majority) behaved like this, but they were an obvious and intrusive presence. I also recall, with embarrassment, the Open Day gimmicks, including toys, branded with the university's name, its logo, and puerile slogans, which were given to everyone who attended.

A recurrent feature of universities' marketing has been the large advertisements, with colour photographs, in newspapers. These have frequently described university events. My belief is that many (or most) of these occasions had been created in order to be described in advertisements and in press releases. At the university where I worked, these events have included, each year, an increasing number of awards ceremonies. I am not referring to graduation ceremonies, at which degrees were conferred on students who had passed exams or written learned theses, but equally formal events at which the university recognised members of its academic and administrative staff who had had exceptional achievements. These included, for lecturers, research successes and teaching skills. Like most of my colleagues, I took little interest in these awards ceremonies.

Each morning, I collected letters and other mail from my pigeon-hole. I remember the day that there was an unusual, sealed envelope addressed to me. It had the university logo and, in red ink, two rubber stamps: 'FROM THE OFFICE OF THE VICE-CHANCELLOR' and 'PRIVATE AND CONFIDENTIAL'. My usual practice was to read some of my mail at the pigeon-holes, while chatting to colleagues who were reading their mail, but I took this letter back to my office and shut the door before opening the envelope. But I had no reason to worry. The letter made me laugh. Then I read it again and I laughed and laughed. But it was not a joke.

The vice-chancellor, and he had signed the letter himself, had invited me to a ceremony at which I would be presented with an award for twenty-five years' service. It was expressed as a summons. The dress code was specified as 'Smart business attire'. I was instructed to be seated at least fifteen minutes before the start of the ceremony. I was requested to be accompanied by my 'spouse (or other significant guest)'. Refreshments would be available after the ceremony.

This letter made me laugh. It seemed to me that the only benefit of this ceremony was to enable the vice-chancellor, and other senior people, to feel important. It was probably not an attempt to buy loyalty, but it could have been. It would certainly have been an opportunity to issue a press release (or paid advertisements) about events at the university, which would be published in newspapers and in other media. This would be seen as a part of the university's marketing efforts.

I am not opposed to the awarding of awards where there is good reason for an award to be awarded, but this made no sense. I felt that I had not done anything that merited a special award. Long service does not always indicate an employee's excellence. It might indicate that there is evidence of persistent incompetence or dishonesty that has discouraged other organisations from offering employment. So, I wrote to the vice-chancellor and said that I was uneasy about this type of award and that I had decided not to attend the awards ceremony. He did not reply. However, I received a telephone call ('off the record') from one of his office staff who did not tell me her name. She sympathised with me and agreed that these awards ceremonies were pointless and wasteful.

One of my colleagues commented that the vice-chancellor 'was again being generous with other people's money and time'.

Many of my students have told me that they regarded the university's marketing as insulting and irritating.

'There's just one thing that annoys me about this university. No, that's not right. There are lots of things that annoy me. But there is one that is particularly annoying.'

'And what is that?'

'The advertisements on the back of buses. Whenever I see one of those, I feel embarrassed to be associated with this university.'

'So do I.'

The university's marketing activity, in which I was required to play a small part, always left me with a sour taste. I felt that it did not paint an accurate picture of the university. In addition, I struggled to believe that it would have the desired effect of increasing enrolments. I was confident that future students would not be fooled by the gimmickry. If I was wrong, and some were fooled, it is difficult to believe that such gullible people would be suited to undergraduate study.

Intense marketing is a consequence of the competition for resources between universities. Unfortunately, marketing activity uses resources, and the benefits might be trivial (or zero). Competition can be wasteful. Ideally, universities would compete to achieve the highest academic standards, but it appears that the usual obvious outcome is that they compete to produce the gimmikiest gimmicks. Lower standards might be necessary to increase enrolment. In tertiary education, there is often a conflict between high standards and profit seeking.

The direct financial costs of universities' marketing activity can be measured and are large. Its indirect financial costs are more difficult to measure but are probably also substantial. Its effects on human behaviour are impossible to measure but are likely to include some degree of alienation of many of the staff and students from the most senior people in their university. It is difficult to believe that the benefits, which also cannot be measured, outweigh the costs.

Although the effects of the social corrosion caused by universities' marketing are difficult to define and its extent is impossible to measure, there is no doubt it exists. It is likely to have long-term effects that are difficult to reverse.

22
Exit from Academia

In 2015, at the age of sixty-seven years, I retired from my university post. I was in excellent health and, although large-scale teaching had become a little more tiring, particularly when I had to present two lectures without a break between them, I was still enjoying academic work, especially the teaching parts of my job. It was always rewarding to help students to understand complex theory and it was especially rewarding when, as a student, I had found the same topics to be difficult. My academic publications continued to please me (although they were never going to make me famous). I decided that I needed a change, and I wanted to have more time for activities that I had neglected, especially contacts with old friends. Claudia had just retired from her teaching work, and I wanted to be able to spend more time with her too.

One of the reasons for deciding to retire was that I did not want to repeat the mistake that, early in my academic career, was made by a colleague. He was in his early sixties. When he returned to work after weeks of illness, his appearance and his stamina had changed. His doctor had told him that he was fit again, but it was clear to all of his colleagues that he was not. He looked old, he tired easily, and he was no longer speaking fluently. He had taught at the same polytechnic for many years, and he was well respected so, of course, his workmates were keen to help him at a difficult time. However, he did not quickly return to good health, and it was not long before his colleagues were commenting on this. 'He's getting the salary, but I'm doing much of the work.' 'He's doing a part-time job and getting a full-time salary.' I promised myself that I would never let this happen to me and that I would retire before my job became too demanding.

The head of my department was taken by surprise when I told him that I had decided to resign. Not only that, he was appalled.

'You can't do that.'

'Why not?'

'Because we need you here.'

'I don't believe that I'm indispensable.'

'But you are. There is nobody else in the department who can hold the attention of more than three hundred students for an hour. And you do it several times a week for the whole of each semester.'

This was the first time that he had made any comment on my teaching skills. I reminded him that I had submitted my letter of resignation.

'But you can withdraw it. And I hope you will.'

I ignored his request. I knew that I wanted to leave full-time academic work. Despite this, when I had retired, I missed it. I missed teaching and I especially missed helping individual students. However, I did not miss university politics. I missed individual colleagues, especially those who had helped me to improve my published work. However, I did not miss being part of an institution in which a significant proportion of the staff did not respect the most senior people. One of the reasons for this widespread disaffection was the intense university marketing. This included the ubiquitous slogans which were a persistent irritant.

The first few weeks of retirement were a strange experience. Each morning, I saw people in cars, on buses, and waiting at bus-stops, all going to their work. I felt that I should have been with them. I felt that I was a fraud. But the mood passed quickly.

Before leaving the university, I emptied the filing cabinets in my office. There were detailed records, on paper, of (mostly complete) research projects. Almost all of this material was handwritten or prepared on a typewriter. This was a reminder of the rapid advance of digital technology. When I started full-time work at this university, in 1987, neither e-mail nor the internet had begun. Word-processing, although seen to be exciting at the time, was, by today's standards, primitive. Further, it was not readily available. When I worked as a Research Assistant from 1970, in my first job after I was awarded my degree, I used punched paper tape and eighty-column punched cards to input data into the university computer. These devices are now of historical interest only (and have been for many years).

Since I retired, my academic writing has been confined to improving and editing existing work. The Nigerian version of my textbook was published in 2019, and its second edition was published in 2021. Updated versions of my articles on the euro and on the Sterling Area have been published in the *Encyclopedia of Economic and Business History*.

Since I left full-time employment, I have enjoyed other kinds of writing. I have found that writing for a non-academic audience is a different process to writing textbooks and academic journal articles. However, I am confident that my academic experience has helped me to develop relevant writing skills.

I have written newspaper articles that are based on my experience as a lecturer. A large proportion of people think they understand how universities function. In these articles, I have described what really happens. People read newspapers (which is why they buy them) and I like the idea of my work being read. It is probable that a significant proportion of my academic articles have not been read by anyone other than the referees. Journals that have published my articles are bought by university libraries in many countries and then bound, shelved, and regularly dusted, but probably rarely read. The number of such journals is, of course, large and increasing, which creates opportunities for unimportant authors (including me) to feel more significant than they are. The printers are able to employ people and to make profits. It's a game where everybody wins (except, of course, the people whose taxes are paid to the universities that finance it).

Some of my stories for young children, which I wrote for Stephen when he was four years old, have been published. This has been satisfying, but my non-academic publication that is of the greatest significance to me is probably *Christine's Man*, my first novel, which was published in 2020. This story is based on my experience as a young lecturer in the 1970s. I wanted to describe my feeling of being surrounded by incompetence and absurdities (and not just at my work). This problem was compounded (and partly caused) by the institutional context. This is a tragi-comic tale which is mostly about my work but also includes other incidents. Examples include interactions with a police officer who did not trust me, and with a (sometimes cantankerous) elderly neighbour who disapproved of me (but also needed me). Christine, an important character in the story, who is based on my memories of Claudia, frequently added to the mix.

The comments that I have received on *Christine's Man* are most encouraging. Some of them are inspiring, but it is difficult to believe that my book deserves these responses. Adjectives have included 'evocative', 'pithy', 'gritty', 'accurate', and 'reminiscent'. A former colleague wrote 'I laughed seventeen times, and I cried twice. But that is not surprising because I was there when it all happened. I was a lecturer at the same polytechnic and at the same time as you. And I had a grumpy old neighbour who was just like yours'.

Several friends have said that the effect of reading *Christine's Man* is that they have decided to write autobiographical fiction. Most of these are the same friends who, when the first of my children's stories was published, said that they were going to write stories for young children (but have not done this). Despite its flaws, which are increasingly obvious to me, having my novel published has been most rewarding.

After nine years, I am still adapting to retirement, but I am enjoying it more and more. I now have grey hair so, despite being neither frail nor disabled, I have often been offered seats on crowded buses. Getting older is a bit like being a teenager again. There have been changes in my anatomy and in my physiology, some of which I did not expect, and, in addition, I am treated differently by other people.

I feel that I am fortunate to have had an academic career, which has been both interesting and rewarding, and from which I have learnt, and am still learning, a great deal (and not just about my subject). My students have been among my best teachers.

Appendix

Chapter 4

My first newspaper article is:
  Jerry Mushin, 'Eligible Liabilities and the Omission of Cash', *The Scotsman*, 21 May 1974.

My first academic article, based on a chapter of my (unsuccessful) thesis, is:
  Jerry Mushin, 'Monetary Policy and Stock-Building in UK Manufacturing', *Bulletin of Economic Research*, Vol 27, No 2, November 1975.

Chapter 6

My first conference presentation is:
  Jerry Mushin and William Samson, 'A Simulation of the Economic Effects of Expenditure Attitudes and Political Structure', in Mark Cross (ed), *Modelling and Simulation in Practice*, Pentech Press, Plymouth, 1979.

Chapter 20

Versions of my textbook are:
  Jerry Mushin, *Income, Interest Rates and Prices*, Dunmore Press, Palmerston North, 1994, 1996,

1999.

Jerry Mushin and Robert Brewer, *Macroeconomics*, Studymates, Taunton, 2001.

Jerry Mushin, *Output and the Role of Money*, World Scientific Publishing Company, New York, 2002.

Jerry Mushin, *Chan Chu He Huo Bi Jue Se Hong Guan Jing Ji Xue Xian Dai Guan Dian*, Hua Xia Chu Ban She, Beijing, 2004. [Translation of *Output and the Role of Money*]

Jerry Mushin, *Interest Rates, Prices, and the Economy*, Scientific Publishers (India), Jodhpur, 2009.

Jerry Mushin, *Prices, Interest Rates, and Aggregate Output*, Tilde University Press, Melbourne, 2015.

Jerry Mushin and Uduakobong Edy-Ewoh, *Output, Prices, and Interest Rates*, Babcock University Press, Ilishan-Remo, 2019, 2021.

For my articles on the Sterling Area and on the euro, published in the *Encyclopedia of Economic and Business History* by the Economic History Association, go to **www.eh.net** and choose **encyclopedia** and then **authors**.

My chapter in a textbook for journalists is:
Jerry Mushin, 'Competing Approaches to Macroeconomic Policy', in Don Milne and John Savage (ed), *Reporting Economics*, New Zealand Journalists Training Organisation, Wellington, 1999.

For abstracts of most of my academic articles, published by the Social Science Research Network, go to **www.ssrn.com**.

Chapter 22

My first novel is:
   Jerry Mushin, *Christine's Man*, Shooting Star Press, Canberra, 2020.

My stories for young children are:
   Jerry Mushin, *Dr Hedgehog and the Post Box Rescue*, Sweet Cherry Publishing, Leicester, 2014.
   Jerry Mushin, *Dr Hedgehog and the Tree Rescue*, Sweet Cherry Publishing, Leicester, 2014.
   Jerry Mushin, *Dr Hedgehog and the River Rescue*, Sweet Cherry Publishing, Leicester, 2014.
   Jerry Mushin, *Dr Hedgehog and the Island Rescue*, Shooting Star Press, Canberra, 2020.

Also published by Piwaiwaka Press

And the Birds Fled to the Bush

Helen Mae Innes

ISBN: 978-1-7385926-7-8

127 x 203mm (5 x 8 in)

Page count: 226

In the ruins of suburbia everyone is just trying to grow and preserve some veggies, catch a fish or deer or two, avoid government officials and their eviction notices, and keep up with the local goss. Meanwhile, Anton, a specialist in birdsong, arrives hoping to conduct research in the surrounding hills. His project is regarded with ire or indifference by all except Tim, a weird loner living in the bush, whose speech is odd and behaviour odder.

An unlikely trio of young men are forced to work together to achieve their different goals in a post-earthquake world. They battle against and work with nature, the officious community board and their absurd proclamations, and a community of hardcase characters.

Not Swinging, Swooning

Stevan Eldred-Grigg

ISBN: 978-1-7385926-6-1

152 x 228mm (6 x 9 in)

Page count: 254

'It's early in the morning,' a boy writes in his diary, 'on the first day of the first year of the most modern decade in the whole of human history. Get in the groove!' The boy, Stevan, is seven years old and one of the middle kids in a nuclear family in a twice-mortgaged new bungalow in a new cul-de-sac in a suburb during the Space Age.

Not Swinging, Swooning is a story about a boy's dreams, dreads, hopes, fears and adventures. A story about elbowing and being elbowed by siblings, aunts, uncles, cousins, neighbours, friends, teachers. A story about pop songs the boy thought were groovy, and about yarns spelled by the olds. A story about being a boy, in a suburb, about becoming, or trying to become, a young man in the mod optimistic hi-gloss world of the sixties of last century.

Harpoon

Hugh Hunter

ISBN: 978-1-7385926-9-2

Size: 152 × 228 mm

(6 × 9in)

Page count: 322

People, place and plot leap to life in this riveting counterfactual thriller set in a war's end New Zealand East Coast c1945. Hugh Hunter exploits to the full the contrast between the sunbaked somnolent township of Harpoon and an unthinkable-until-it-happened assault landing by an undercover German detachment on a mystery mission. Ranick, Klaske, Tripp, Bluey Totoro, the Weatherby sisters and a host of other characters, German, Pākehā and Māori, lodge in the reader's mind long after the last page is turned. The assault climaxes with guns blazing and scores settled in a scene worthy of the best thriller writers.
Malcolm McKinnon